High School Leaders And Their Schools

Volume II:

Profiles of Effectiveness

Leonard O. Pellicer

Lorin W. Anderson

James W. Keefe

Edgar A. Kelley

Lloyd E. McCleary

National Association of Secondary School Principals
1904 Association Drive ● Reston, Virginia 22091

Scott D. Thomson, NASSP Executive Director
Thomas F. Koerner, Director of Publications
Patricia Lucas George, Editor
Eugenia Cooper Potter, Technical Editor

IBSN: 0-88210-238-9

The Research Team
Leonard O. Pellicer is professor in the Department of Educational Leadership and Policies, University of South Carolina.
Lorin W. Anderson is research professor in the Department of Educational Leadership and Policies, University of South Carolina.
James W. Keefe is director of research, National Association of Secondary School Principals.
Edgar A. Kelley is professor in the Department of Educational Leadership, Western Michigan University.
Lloyd E. McCleary is professor of educational administration, University of Utah.

The Steering Committee
Patricia Campbell, Lakewood Senior High School, Lakewood, Colorado
Glen M. DeHaven, Oldtown School, Oldtown, Maryland
Richard A. Gorton, University of Wisconsin-Milwaukee
Jacqueline H. Simmons, Paul Robeson High School, Chicago, Illinois
Norman O. Stevens, Mill River Union High School, North Clarendon, Vermont
Michael K. Thomas, Vashon High School, St. Louis, Missouri
Peggy P. Walters, J. Frank Dobie High School, Houston, Texas
Gary P. Wells, Henley High School, Klamath Falls, Oregon
Jeannette M. Wheatley, Cass Technical High School, Detroit, Michigan
James V. Wright, Fremont Ross High School, Fremont, Ohio

CONTENTS

Tables

Preface

We can be assured that effective leadership is important to the success of schools. A decade of research confirms that view.

Less certain, however, is our understanding of the characteristics and behavior of high performing principals and of their administrative and programmatic procedures.

This study, *Profiles of Effectiveness,* brings us much closer to a comprehension of the critical behaviors and management tendencies of competent principals. It moves beyond generalities, to definitive profiles. It manages the complexities of the question and provides some clean results. It provides solid data upon which to build stronger principalship preparation programs and evaluation systems. In short, this work advances our understanding of the unique role of the principal in a school setting.

A special note of appreciation goes to the research team for this significant study: Leonard O. Pellicer, Lorin W. Anderson, James W. Keefe, Edgar A. Kelley, and Lloyd E. McCleary. All are distinguished educators in their own right. Together they make a formidable team.

A study committee of 10 persons helped to define the research questions and to develop the program design. These five principals, four assistant principals, and one university professor were invaluable to the success of the project.

The NASSP intends to make available to the education community and to the interested citizen, a flow of significant information about principals and schools. With this volume, I feel that we have succeeded admirably in this quest.

Scott D. Thomson
Executive Director
NASSP

Introduction

The introduction to Volume I of NASSP's comprehensive study of the high school principalship in 1978 included the statement, "The principalship today is not the principalship of 1965, nor will it be the principalship of 1985." These words underscore the dynamic nature of the senior high school principalship and form the basis for the NASSP's enduring commitment to regular and systematic monitoring of the principalship through major studies of the kind reported in the following pages.

This study is the third in a series of national studies of the high school principalship dating back to the early 1960s. Each study has represented an attempt to build a knowledge base about the senior high school principalship by systematically gathering, organizing, and presenting a large amount of descriptive data and then investigating several important aspects of the principalship not yet fully explored.

The major purpose of this study was to analyze and describe high school leaders and their schools. The focus of the present study has been broadened beyond that of its antecedents to include both the major roles in building administration: the principalship and the assistant principalship. For the first time, descriptive data have been gathered, analyzed, and reported about principals and assistant principals in the same schools. This expanded treatment represents researchers' awareness of the complexity of the principalship and the importance of the entire administrative team that functions together to organize, administer, and lead American high schools.

The research questions that guided the study were:

1. What are the personal and professional characteristics, job-related tasks, and expectations of senior high school principals and assistant principals?
2. What similarities and differences exist in the characteristics, tasks, and expectations of principals and assistant principals considering grade levels administered and selected demographic characteristics of the schools?
3. What are the characteristics of senior high school staffs, students, and communities?
4. What variations exist in senior high school organizational structures and instructional programs?
5. What similarities and differences exist in senior high school programs considering grade level organization and selected demographic characteristics of the schools?
6. What are the views of senior high school principals and assistant principals on selected educational issues and trends?

1

7. What indices (characteristics and behaviors) of high performing and typically performing principals are related to school effectiveness?

8. What are the administrative and programmatic similarities and differences between effective schools administered by principals described as "high performers" and those administered by "typical" principals?

Answers to the first six questions are reported in Volume I of the study. Questions 7 and 8 are explored in this volume.

Design of the Study

The study was conducted by a research team with the advice and assistance of a steering committee composed of four senior high school assistant principals, three large-school senior high principals, two small-school senior high principals, and a professor of educational leadership. The research team and steering committee met together during the early stages of the study to discuss objectives, clarify research questions, and review the survey instruments for phase I of the study. School selection and site visit protocols for the second phase of the study were developed by the research team in response to a study design proposed by the NASSP research department.

Several researchers generously assisted in the actual site visits and in preparing the case studies for this volume: Joella Gipson-Simpson, professor of education at Wayne State University, Detroit, Michigan; Paul W. Hersey, director of professional assistance at NASSP, Reston, Virginia; Jennifer Kranz, University of Utah; Richard Spradling, University of South Carolina; and Kenneth R. Stevenson, University of South Carolina.

Organization of the Report

Unquestionably, senior high school administrators occupy positions of critical importance in the nation's schools. What these persons do and how they manage to meet their innumerable responsibilities are of vital interest to aspiring school leaders, current practitioners, professors of preservice programs, and officials who establish certification guidelines. The data presented in this report offer a picture of American high school leaders and their schools in 1988.

Chapter I presents a discussion of the study's purpose and design. Chapter II is devoted to quantitative comparisons on the entire sample, while Chapters III, IV, and V offer a picture of findings from school site visits. The final chapter presents a summary of the findings and selected recommendations for future research.

I Purpose and Design

In recent years, two major changes have taken place in the way in which the high school principalship is perceived by those who study it. First, the principalship has been linked to school effectiveness. Principals, by using proper management techniques and leadership strategies, particularly in curriculum and instruction, are expected to have a dramatic impact on the effectiveness of their schools (Keefe, 1987; Dwyer, 1986; Hallinger and Murphy, 1985; Ogawa and Hart, 1985; Walberg and Lane, 1985). Second, the principalship is more often spoken of as a collaborative responsibility, the individual called the principal and key associates, collectively known as the administrative team or supervisory-management team (Gorton and Kattman, 1985; Greenfield, 1985; Marshall, 1985; Reed and Himmler, 1985; Georgiades et al., 1979; Trump, 1977).

While these changes are evident in the professional literature, little in the way of "hard data" or empirical evidence is available to establish the extent to which changes have found their way into practice. The purpose of this study is to increase our knowledge about the composition and operation of the administrative team and our understanding of how that team addresses the issues of organization and school effectiveness. Specifically, the study attempts to answer three basic questions.

The first question is "How are administrative teams organized and how do they solve problems and make decisions?" To probe this question, the research team for this study focused on the decision-making models that were (or were not) operating in the schools, the strategies used to identify and address several actual school problems, the schools' formal and informal leadership structures, and the means by which tasks were assigned and authority delegated.

The second question is "What is the administrative team's definition of instructional leadership and how is it operationalized?" To explore this question, the researchers asked the members of each school's administrative team to summarize their major accomplishments, both in general, as well as relating to curriculum and instruction in particular. Administrative team members were asked to describe the best teachers in their schools, their conception of instructional leadership, and their views on the purpose of schooling.

The third question is "How does the administrative team achieve optimum productivity and satisfaction?" Assuming that effective schools

3

are those in which a balance between productivity (student achievement and success) and satisfaction (teacher and student attitudes) has been realized, the researchers were interested in ways that the administrative team had achieved or failed to achieve this balance. The researchers were interested in administrative team members' definitions of success, their indicators or measures of success, their attempts at balancing concerns for excellence and equity, and their methods of dealing with increased external regulation.

A plan for the study was developed to address these questions. The plan included the selection of schools to be visited, the methods to be used by researchers in collecting the data in each school, and the format for presenting and discussing the collected data. Each of these components of the plan is discussed in the following sections.

Selection of Schools

The original population from which the sites to be visited were selected consisted of schools whose current principal had participated in the NASSP Assessment Center (NASSP, 1986) and in the field testing of the NASSP Comprehensive Assessment of School Environments (CASE) battery (Halderson et al., 1989).

Some further background on the NASSP Assessment Center and on the CASE battery are pertinent to our discussion.

In 1975, NASSP, with the technical assistance of the American Psychological Association, devised an Assessment Center plan to assist school districts in identifying and developing skilled school leaders. The project required four years of research and a three-year validation study conducted by Neil Schmidt of Michigan State University. The validation study showed a positive predictive validity for the NASSP Assessment Center, with ratings tied to principals' performance on the job. More than 50 Assessment Centers are now operating in the United States, Canada, England, West Germany, and Australia.

The NASSP Assessment Center materials use behavior modeling as their chief training strategy, incorporating rehearsal and reinforcement during simulations of school district problems and activities. Assessment center activities provide (a) *participants* with information about their own strengths and weaknesses, (b) *school districts* with objective assessments of participants' readiness to assume administrative responsibilities, and (c) *district administrators* with data for use in planning inservice activities. The capabilities assessed in participants include problem analysis, judgment, organizational ability, decisiveness, leadership, sensitivity, motivation, stress tolerance, educational values, and oral and written communication skills. Participants engage in leaderless group activities, fact-facting and stress exercises, and paper-and-pencil "in-basket" tasks dealing with school problems. NASSP supplies materials and trains administrators as assessors in support of the project. (See Appendix A.)

4

The Comprehensive Assessment of School Environments (CASE) battery was developed by NASSP from 1982 to 1985, to delineate the various components of a Task Force model on school environments. Such effectiveness variables as school climate, student satisfaction, and productivity were found to have multiple, interacting determinants, including inputs from the societal environment, the school district environment, and the community environment. These inputs included the goals, characteristics, and attitudes of individuals, groups, and organizations. The CASE model provides a framework for depicting the relationships and outcomes from the interaction of these determinants. (See Appendix B.)

In 1987, James Keefe of NASSP collected data from 29 schools and Neil Schmidt of Michigan State University analyzed the data to determine the model's component linkages. The pilot study and a later normative study indicated that societal features such as ideologies and structures of dominance (i.e., wealth, social class, or occupational hierarchy) influence the values and organizational characteristics of the school district. These, in turn, influence the operation of the school and the attitudes and values of school personnel. All these interactively affect the perceptions of teachers, students, and parents toward school climate. These perceptions of climate also relate to student satisfaction and productivity. It should be noted for purposes of clarity that the CASE model defines school climate as an enduring pattern of shared perceptions about the characteristics of an organization and its members, while satisfaction is viewed as the subject's individual affective response to his or her own particular environment ("I like or feel good about . . . "). CASE data were collected from questionnaires completed by principals, teachers, and students. (See Appendix C.)

A sample of 74 principals was selected from the NASSP Assessor training program population. The assumption behind this strategy was that principals selected as assessors would be at least average in their own Assessment Center ratings. The principals of 37 of these schools were rated well above average in assessor skills. The principals of the other 37 schools were about average. (No principals with below average ratings were included in the sample. An outlier study was not the goal.)

CASE data were collected from each of these 74 schools. Regrettably, when time came for the actual selection of schools to be visited, only data for variables reported on optical-scan answer sheets were available to the research team. Certain other data supplied by the principals (including achievement test results) were not yet entered into the computer files. The additional time needed to enter and profile these data would, in effect, have postponed the study for an entire school year.

Data on only eight variables, then, were considered in deciding to visit particular schools. These variables were the number of years the principal had been at the school (YRSEXP); the percentage of students in remedial and college preparatory programs (REMED, COLLPREP); the climate of the school as perceived by teachers and students (TCLIM, SCLIM); the degree of satisfaction expressed by teachers as well as students (TSAT, SSAT); and the classification of the principals based on their NASSP assessor program ratings (with "A" principals scoring above average and "B" principals scoring about average).

Early in the planning process, the research team decided to visit four schools with "A" principals and four with "B" principals. The team agreed that the principals selected should have served as principals of their respective schools a minimum of two years. (In actuality, seven of the eight principals visited had held their positions at least five years.) After these initial considerations were met, the actual choice of schools was based on the remaining six CASE variables.

Two "benchmark" schools were initially selected. The first school (number 78) had an "A" principal, fewer students than the sample average in the remedial program, and a greater than average percentage of students in the college preparatory program. The school scores on the Teacher Climate, Teacher Satisfaction, Student Climate, and Student Satisfaction scales were well above average (in the highest quarter of the distribution of 74 schools). This school represented the "upper bound" of principal and school effectiveness.

The second "benchmark" school (number 137) had a "B" principal. Slightly more than the average percentage of students were enrolled in the remedial program (20 to 29 percent), with an average percentage in the college preparatory program. The school scores on the Teacher Climate, Teacher Satisfaction, Student Climate, and Student Satisfaction scales were much lower than average (in the lowest quarter of the distribution of 74 schools). This school represented our "lower bound" of principal and school effectiveness.

The remaining six schools were selected because their data profiles were intriguing to the researchers. The first three schools all had "A" principals. One school (number 18) had a smaller percentage of students enrolled in the college preparatory program, but the overall student climate and satisfaction scores were well above average. The teacher climate and satisfaction scores were about average. Another school (number 39) had fewer students in the remedial program and more students in the college preparatory program, but both teacher and student satisfaction scores were much lower than the average. A third school (number 2) very much resembled our "upper bound" school but its student population was more representative of the other schools in the sample. From 10 to 19 percent of the students were enrolled in the remedial program, with from 50 to 69 percent in the college preparatory program. The Teacher Climate, Teacher Satisfaction, Student Climate, and Student Satisfaction scores were quite similar to those in the "upper bound" school.

The remaining three schools had "B" principals. School number 72 was selected because of an interesting student population and anomalous climate and satisfaction scores. A smaller than average percentage of students was enrolled in both the remedial and college preparatory programs (suggesting a large vocational program). Teacher Climate and Student Satisfaction scores were well above average, but Teacher Satisfaction and Student Climate scores were only average. School number 101 was chosen because of varying perceptions between teachers and students. Teacher Climate and Satisfaction scores fell in the normal range, but Student Climate and Satisfaction scores were higher than average. An average percentage of students were enrolled in the remedial and college preparatory programs. School number 131, like school 101, showed interesting differences between teacher and student perceptions. Teacher Climate scores were well below average, but Student Satisfaction scores were higher than average. The Teacher Climate scores were particularly intriguing in view of a larger than average percentage of students enrolled in the college preparatory program.

A summary of the data on schools selected for site visits is included in Table 1.1. The schools are listed in terms of the principal's classification (A vs. B), the years of experience of each principal in the school, and the relative standing of each school on the remaining six variables. The percentage of students in the remedial program, percentage of students in the college preparatory program, teacher climate, teacher satisfaction, student climate, and student satisfaction scores are indicated by pluses ($+$), minuses (-), and pivots (∇). (The meaning of these symbols is explained in the key below the table.)

TABLE 1.1
Summary of Schools Selected for Site Visits

SCHOOL	PRINCIPAL	YRSEXP	REMED	COLLPREP	TCLIM	TSAT	SCLIM	SSAT
002	A	8+	∇	∇	+	+	+	+
018	A	5–8	∇	—	∇	∇	+	+
039	A	8+	—	+	∇	—	∇	—
078	A	5–8	—	+	+	+	+	+
072	B	5–8	—	—	+	∇	∇	+
101	B	8+	∇	∇	∇	∇	+	+
131	B	8+	∇	+	—	∇	∇	+
137	B	2–3	+	∇	—	—	—	—
AVERAGES		5–8	10–19	50–69	42–45	26–31	37–42	56–60

Key: The SCHOOL code is an arbitrarily assigned identification number. PRINCIPAL is the category to which the principal of the school was assigned based on his or her performance in NASSP assessor training, with A = principals scoring well above average and B = principals scoring about average. YRSEXP is the number of years (given as a range) that a principal has served as principal of that school. REMED is the percentage of students enrolled in a remedial instruction program. COLLPREP is the percentage of students enrolled in a college preparatory program. TCLIM is the total score on the Teacher Climate scale; TSAT is the total score on the Teacher Satisfaction scale. SCLIM is the total score on the Student Climate scale; SSAT is the total score on the Student Satisfaction scale. The AVERAGE for YRSEXP is the median range; for REMED, and COLLPREP, the median percentiles; the AVERAGES for TCLIM, TSAT, SCLIM, and SSAT are semi-interquartile ranges (within which 50 percent of the schools fall on these variables). The symbol "∇" indicates that the schools scored average on that variable; "+" and "-" indicate scores well above or below the average, respectively.

Methods Used To Collect the Data

Each school was visited by two researchers for a period of three days. The research team prepared five interview protocols to be used during the visits. The first three sets of protocols were intended for use with members of the administrative team (principals, assistant principals, guidance counselors, etc.). These protocols focused on the three research questions guiding the study (see Appendix D). The fourth protocol (Appendix E) was prepared for use with teachers; the fifth (Appendix F), for parents.

The site visitors were instructed to focus on the three primary research questions. They were to collect whatever information or evidence was needed to answer these three questions. The protocols were intended to assist that effort, not narrowly circumscribe it. The protocols served as guidelines rather than mandates.

Each site visit began with an extensive interview of the principal. During this initial interview, the researchers became familiar with the physical layout of the school and the organization of the administrative team. They posed the basic questions in the first three interview protocols and set the agenda for the remainder of the visit.

During the visit, the researchers met with each member of the administrative team, a minimum of two groups of teachers, and, as appropriate, one or more groups of parents. Classrooms were visited and student groups interviewed. The classroom visits and student interviews were unstructured, with each researcher making notes of his or her impressions and perceptions. Archival data such as test scores, and minutes of meetings and exhibits (bulletin boards, trophy cases) were examined.

Format for Presenting and Discussing the Data

Following each site visit, a case study was prepared for each school by the researchers who visited it. A common organizational format was adopted for the preparation of each case. The opening section presented a profile of the school and the surrounding community. The next three sections reported on the three primary research questions, and were labeled "Administrative Team and Decision Making," "Instructional Leadership," and "Productivity and Satisfaction." The final section offered a summary and any conclusions drawn by the pairs of researchers.

The compendium of case studies was distributed to members of the original research team for purposes of preparing cross-case analyses. Each member of the research team was directed to examine the case studies in terms of one of the major research questions. The cross-case analyses were intended to review and summarize the similarities and differences among sites, prepare appropriate and defensible responses to the research questions, and suggest any implications for the improvement of the principalship that could be derived from the evidence gathered. The results of these cross-case analyses are presented in Chapters III, IV, and V of this volume.

Summary

The study was designed to further our understanding of the organization and operation of high school administrative teams, the nature of instructional leadership provided by these teams, and their concerns for productivity and satisfaction. A vast amount of data was collected by the researchers during three-day site visits of eight schools. The schools were selected because previously collected data suggested that they were interesting and potentially informative sites. Following the visits, the researchers prepared a series of case studies that summarized the evidence gathered. Finally, cross-case analyses were developed to address three primary research questions:

1. How are administrative teams organized and how do they solve problems and make decisions?

2. What is the administrative team's definition of instructional leadership and how is it operationalized?

3. How does the administrative team achieve optimum productivity and satisfaction?

II Quantitative Comparisons

Data were available from NASSP's Comprehensive Assessment of School Environments (CASE) battery (Schmitt and Doherty, 1988) for all 74 schools of the larger initial sample. Comparisons could be made among these schools on variables other than those which were the focus of the site visits. In this chapter, schools are compared by principal categories ("A" and "B"), and by higher and lower levels of student achievement, satisfaction, and success on a large number of variables. These variables, in 32 major categories and more than 80 in all, include school goals and policies, the allocation and use of resources, the amount of regulation and autonomy, teacher commitment and stress, and principal performance and reaction to change.

The Identification of Effective Schools

The members of the research team decided to define school effectiveness in terms of three variables: student achievement, student satisfaction, and student success. Student achievement was measured by students' combined scores on standardized tests of reading and mathematics. The mean percentile ranks for reading and mathematics for students at all grade levels within a school were computed and the mean of these means was used as an indicator of the school's achievement. Student satisfaction was measured by students' responses to a short form of the NASSP Student Satisfaction Survey in the CASE battery. The response options to these items ranged from 1 to 5, with 5 being the most positive or satisfying response. The responses were averaged across all items for each student, and then across all students in each school to obtain an average student satisfaction score for that school. Finally, student success was defined as the percentage of students in the school who received passing grades in all their courses.

The mean scores, standard deviations, minimum score, and maximum score for these three effectiveness variables are shown in Table 2.1. The average student achievement score in the average school of the sample was 61.83. This score means that the average student in the average school had a combined reading and mathematics score equal to or higher than approximately 62 percent of some hypothetical national student population. The range of achievement was from an average 24th percentile to an average just below the 92nd percentile. (Note: These are rough estimates of student achievement. Different schools used different

TABLE 2.1
Summary of Effectiveness Variables

Effectiveness Variable	n	Mean	Std Dev	Min	Max
Student Achievement (percentile)	74	61.83	14.46	24.0	91.75
Student Satisfaction (1–5 scale)	74	3.23	0.18	2.79	3.81
Student Success (percentage)	74	88.01	15.30	8.00	100.00

tests of achievement at different grade levels to compute school averages. For this reason, it was not possible to establish exact comparability for student achievement.)

The average student satisfaction score in the average school was 3.23. Assuming that a score of 3 on a five-point scale represents a neutral reaction, this average satisfaction score indicated that the average student in the average school was at least somewhat satisfied. The range across schools was much narrower than for achievement, with the most positive mean at 3.81 and the most negative at 2.79.

The average student success score was 88.01. Almost 90 percent of the students in the average school passed all the courses in which they were enrolled. At the extremes, however, only 8 percent of the students in one school passed all courses, while all students in several schools passed every course.

Correlations among the three school effectiveness variables were computed. None of these correlations were statistically significant ($p < 0.05$), the largest being a *negative* 0.127 between satisfaction and success. The correlations of achievement with satisfaction and success were -0.003 and 0.076, respectively. It would seem that these three measures of school effectiveness are quite independent.

Because of notable differences among schools in their student populations, a decision was made *not* to use the unconverted measures of student achievement, student satisfaction, and student success as direct measures of school effectiveness. Rather, a series of regression analyses were performed to predict the achievement, satisfaction, and success scores of each school that could be expected given the student populations and other relevant variables.

Two criteria were used to select variables for the initial regression analyses. First, the variables had to be relatively stable over time. Sudden changes in the variables were unlikely to occur. This criterion provided some stability to the estimates of expected achievement, satisfaction, and success. Second, the variables were derived from the responses of principals or teachers, *not* students. Variables derived from student responses would likely have confounded the interpretation of the regression results since the dependent variables (i.e., achievement, satisfaction) were measured with student instruments. Variables derived from the same self-report instruments typically have spuriously high correlations.

Separate regression analyses were performed for the three school effectiveness variables. Variables that entered the regression equation at or near the 0.05 level of significance were retained. Three variables were used to predict the expected *achievement* level for each school. These variables (with their significance levels) were the percentage of students eligible for free or reduced-price lunch (0.006), the availability of budgeted resources (0.009), and the percentage of students in the remedial program (0.060). In combination, these three variables accounted for 33.8 percent of the variance in student achievement across schools.

Four variables were used to predict the average *satisfaction* of the students in each school. These variables were teacher commitment (0.002), the dropout rate of the school (0.014), the amount of vandalism that occurred in the school (0.020), and the age of the school building (0.063). In combination, these four variables accounted for 35.6 percent of the variance in student satisfaction across schools.

No variables were found to be reliably associated with student success. Student success may, in fact, be a within-school variable. The meaning of student success as conceptualized in this study may be idiosyncratic to each school, with predictable percentages of students in every school receiving As, Bs, and so on. The high success rate and the results of the correlational analyses lend support to this hypothesis. Since between-school analyses of within-school variables are unlikely to yield much meaningful information, student success was dropped from all further consideration.

Expected mean scores were calculated for each school based on the regression equations for student achievement and student satisfaction. These expected mean scores were subtracted from the actual mean scores to generate residual achievement and satisfaction scores for each school. The interpretation of these residual scores is quite straightforward; in general, the higher the residual score, the more effective the school. If, for example, the residual achievement score was positive, then the achievement of the students was higher than expected, given their economic status, their school program, and the amount of resources allocated to various programs and activities. Similarly, if the residual satisfaction score was negative, the satisfaction of the students was lower than expected, given the commitment of their teachers, the dropout rate in the school, the amount of vandalism, and the age of the school building.

On the basis of these residual achievement scores, schools were allocated to one of three achievement categories. They were also placed in one of three satisfaction categories based on their residual satisfaction scores. These three achievement and satisfaction categories represented schools scoring well above expectation, schools scoring well below expectation, and schools scoring at or near their expected placement. Placement in these categories was quite independent because of the near-zero correlation of achievement and satisfaction.

Each school was evaluated in three separate categories, including one based on the principal's performance in the NASSP assessor training program. The first category represented the type of principal, the second the achievement of the students, and the third the satisfaction of the students. The schools were compared by categories on a number of variables (termed "explanatory variables"). These explanatory variables, as well as the outcome and predictor variables described above, are shown in Appendix F.

The inclusion of three quite independent outcome variables in the analysis suggested that a three-way analysis of variance (ANOVA) would be the most obvious statistical procedure for comparisons among schools. Two categories for principals, and three categories each for achievement and satisfaction, however, would have required means and variances in 18 cells. If an equal distribution of schools for each of the three categorical variables were assumed, then only about four schools per cell would be included in the analysis. To increase the count per cell, two two-way ANOVAs were performed instead (PRINCIPAL x ACHIEVEMENT and PRINCIPAL x SATISFACTION). The results of these analyses are discussed in the following sections.

Principal Effectiveness

Differences between the two groups of principals were examined in two analyses. Statistically significant differences between the two groups were found on only 12 of the more than 80 variables in the analyses. All these differences involved three clusters of variables: the principal's perceptions of school goals, the principal's participation in decision making, and the principal's reactions to change.

● *Perceptions of School Goals*

Type "B" principals were more likely to support the importance of 4 of the 14 goals in the principal's CASE instrument. These goals were:

1. increasing the skills of students

2. increasing the cost-effectiveness of programs

3. developing methods to maximize the use of school time

4. increasing parent and community involvement.

Type "A" principals were less likely to endorse the importance of any of these goals.

● *Participation in Decision Making*

Type "A" principals were more likely to be involved in two kinds of decisions: policy decisions and program decisions. No differences emerged

13

in the involvement of the two groups in personnel decisions (i.e., hiring and promotion).

● *Reactions to Change*

In general, type "B" principals were more positively predisposed to change than were type "As." "Bs" were more likely to agree with the following statements than their type "A" counterparts:

1. Our school staff tries to understand the needs of our students.
2. We try to find out how the people who will be affected feel about proposed new programs.
3. We carefully evaluate our programs.
4. Our administrators and teachers are open to student or parent suggestions.

No differences were found in any of the other outcome, predictor, or explanatory variables listed in Appendix F. Specifically, the two groups of principals did not differ on such variables as the allocation of resources, autonomy, years in the principalship, or ratings of their performance. Furthermore, they showed no differences in relation to teacher commitment, teacher stress, teacher adjustment, teacher satisfaction, student residual satisfaction, or student residual achievement.

Student Residual Achievement

Only 5 differences among the three groups of schools classified by student residual achievement were statistically significant ($p < 0.05$). Since some 80 variables were examined, 5 such differences would almost be expected by chance. Nonetheless, these 5 variables are described briefly.

Three differences were connected with the ratings of principal performance. Principals of those schools in which the students achieved about as well as expected were rated more positively in their direction of student behavior and their maintenance of the school plant than were principals of the other two groups. Principals of "as well as expected" schools were also rated more positively in their direction of support services than were the principals of schools whose students had higher achievement than expected.

Principals of the "as well as expected" schools were less likely to use their resources for public information and community relations than were principals of schools with student achievement lower than expected. Principals of schools in which student achievement was higher than expected fell in between but did not differ significantly from the other groups.

Finally, schools in which students achieved as well as expected were more likely to have strict policies governing student employment than were schools in the other two groups. Once again, the schools in the two extreme groups did not differ significantly in this regard.

Interestingly, the three categories of schools did not differ on such variables as the goals set by the principals, the principal's participation in decision making, the use of resources for various purposes (with the exception of community relations mentioned above), the degree to which curriculum guidance and supervision were provided, the amount of district regulation, the number of professional staff members, or the principal's reactions to change. Nor did the groups differ on teacher commitment, teacher stress, teacher adjustment, teacher climate, teacher satisfaction, student climate, or student satisfaction.

Student Residual Satisfaction

Eight statistically significant satisfaction differences were identified among the three categories of schools. Once again, considering that more than 80 variables were examined, 8 statistically significant differences were only a few more than would be expected by chance. Nevertheless, we will summarize them briefly.

Four of the satisfaction differences concerned school goals as perceived by principals. Principals of schools in which student satisfaction was higher than expected were *less* likely than the principals of the other two groups to see the following goals as important:

1. Enhancing the school athletic program
2. Upgrading programs for special students
3. Upgrading vocational programs.

Furthermore, principals of these "higher than expected" schools were less likely than principals of schools in which students were about as satisfied as expected to see the importance of achieving racial integration as a goal. The principals of schools whose students were less satisfied than expected fell somewhere in the middle on this issue, but did not differ significantly from either of the other two groups.

Two of the satisfaction differences among these three groups of schools concerned the degree to which district policy required adherence in the areas of instruction and evaluation. Principals of schools whose students were about as satisfied as expected indicated higher degrees of district regulation of evaluation than the other two groups. These same principals also reported higher degrees of district regulation of instruction than principals in schools with less satisfied students. Principals of schools whose students were more satisfied than expected fell somewhere in between, but did not differ significantly from the other two categories.

Another difference among these groups of schools emerged in regard to principal participation in decision making. Principals whose students were about as satisfied as expected indicated more frequent participation in policy decisions than principals of schools whose students were less

15

satisfied. Principals of schools in which students were more satisfied than expected fell somewhere in between.

The final difference among these three groups concerned principals' reactions to change. Principals of schools in which student satisfaction was about as expected were more likely to agree that their school programs were carefully evaluated than were principals whose student satisfaction was less than expected. Principals of the more satisfied schools were somewhere in between.

Again, the three groups of schools did not differ on any of the other outcomes or explanatory variables in Appendix F. Clearly, there are more similarities among the schools than differences.

Principals in Different Categories of Schools

The analysis of the data permitted an examination of the interaction between principals and schools—whether certain principal differences existed only in particular categories of schools. A few statistically significant interactions were located and are enumerated below.

1. In schools where students had higher satisfaction scores than expected, type "B" principals were more likely than their type "A" counterparts to endorse the goals of upgrading (a) programs for exceptional students, (b) programs and practices for student discipline, and (c) their college preparatory and other academic programs. Differences between the two groups of principals did not emerge in the other satisfaction categories.

2. In schools with lower satisfaction scores than expected, type "B" principals were more likely to enforce student attendance rules. In these same schools, type "B" principals were more likely to agree that the staff tries to understand student needs. These differences between the two groups of principals were not evident in the other satisfaction categories.

3. In schools where students had higher than expected achievement scores, type "A" principals were more likely to enforce student attendance rules than their type "B" counterparts. Interestingly, the reverse was true in schools with lower than expected student achievement; i.e., type "B" principals in those schools were more likely to enforce student attendance rules than were type "A" principals.

4. In schools whose students had higher than expected achievement scores, type "B" principals were more likely to be comfortable with current programs than type "A" principals. No difference were noted between the groups of principals in the other two achievement categories.

5. Schools with higher than expected student achievement evidenced higher teacher commitment when type "B" principals headed the school. Conversely, in schools where students achieved about as well as expected, teacher commitment was higher when type "A" principals were in charge. This same pattern held for teacher satisfaction.

6. In schools where students had lower than expected achievement, student perceptions of school climate were more positive when type "B"

16

principals headed the school. Conversely, schools with average student achievement reported more positive student perceptions of school climate under type "A" principals.

7. In schools where students achieved about as well as expected, teacher perceptions of school climate were more positive under type "A" principals. Conversely, in both other achievement categories, teacher perceptions of school climate were more positive under type "B" principals.

8. Schools whose students achieved as well as expected had higher student satisfaction when type "A" principals were in charge. Conversely, the other two categories of schools had higher student satisfaction under type "B" principals.

Implications

The results of these supplementary analyses are far from clearcut. Correlations between principal performance in NASSP assessor training and specific aspects of school effectiveness are not very helpful, especially when effectiveness is measured against expectations in particular situations. It would appear that both types of principals, "A" and "B," must be judged in the context of their school populations and local environments. Perhaps skill in administrator assessment is not a good proxy for actual performance in school management. Assessing skills in others is not the same as applying skills effectively in real school settings.

The following chapters report principal and administrative team performance in the actual environments of the sample schools.

III The Administrative Team

The administrative team has become an essential part of many schools. Principals have arrived at their interpretation of administrative team organization and function either quite deliberately or have developed it out of necessity. Both versions are represented in the sample of schools for this study. No standard version exists of the administrative team concept and the practices associated with its effective use. Many principals are forced to create their own models under circumstances that are less than ideal. The research team examined several models and associated practices in this sample of eight secondary schools. The goal was to provide a guide for principals and to establish a basis for further research to advance understanding about the place and function of the administrative team in secondary schools.

The administrative team is not a new organizational approach in schools. Most of the literature, however, concerns district level organization (Haderman, 1988). Literature on school-level administrative teams is largely composed of accounts of single school efforts or of conceptual treatments discussing how schools might employ teams (Anderson, 1988; Wilhelm, 1984). The NASSP study reported here relies on intensive site visits conducted by external investigators, carefully prepared data-gathering protocols, and school documents such as policy statements, agendas and minutes, school publications, descriptive reports, etc. Case studies of each school were prepared from these sources. This analysis is based on the case studies and the supporting documents.

Three research questions (see Chapter I) guided the overall study. The first question dealt with the administrative team: "How are administrative teams organized, and how do they solve problems and make decisions?" This question was addressed in terms of sub-questions about team composition and functions, formal and informal leadership structures, planning, decision making, and problem-solving practices, variations among schools, and the principal's role. Individual and group interview protocols and previously gathered data guided the researchers' observations and examination of records at each site.

Administrative Teams: Composition and Functions

In our sample of schools, the administrative team always included the assistant principal(s), and often other key staff members such as a counselor, a department chair, a teacher representative or union building representative, or the director of activities or athletics. (In the larger schools of 1,400 students or more, an assistant principal was directly responsible for counseling services or activities/athletics.) Additional teachers, usually elected, sometimes were members. Size and composition of the administrative team appeared to be directly related to constituencies and followed the management principle of functional representation (instructional departments, student services, activities, teacher welfare, etc.).

Two factors affecting team operation, in addition to school size, were the degree of formal status accorded the team, and the extent of delegation of authority. Some schools operated in a highly formal fashion, with regularly scheduled meetings, agenda and minutes, announcement of actions taken, and a formal policy about membership and attendance. Others operated on call of the principal, without published agenda, and decisions were announced in regularly circulated minutes and bulletins. Formal meetings in all cases were held either weekly or bi-weekly. The frequency and content of meetings seemed to depend on the extent of informal contact among team members. In one case, team members were located in the same area of the building. The amount of daily contact among team members precluded any need to meet formally except for actions that crossed areas of authority, to review assignments and evaluate performance, to examine reports such as student test scores or teacher evaluations, and to consider serious schoolwide problems.

In all cases, team members, particularly assistant principals, were delegated specific areas of responsibility with specified authority for taking action. In one school, for example, three assistant principals were each assigned curriculum areas (including the evaluation of teachers in those areas), administrative functions (scheduling, attendance, discipline, activities, etc.), and specific personnel to supervise. Each had a budget to manage and was responsible for planning and other administrative functions. Only when actions were not specifically delegated or demanded that others be informed were matters brought to the team. Weekly team meetings were devoted first to reports of actions that might be informative to others before additional items were raised. In other schools, however, individuals or teams were expected to meet informally before scheduled team meetings to iron out differences and to form proposals. In this way, few conflicts occurred that required negotiation during team meetings.

In every instance, principals reserved veto power over team decisions. As one principal stated, "The principal has one more vote. When I feel strongly I go ahead and asked them to bear with me." This principal and others were very sensitive to a "zone of tolerance" and worked with the administrative team to develop a working consensus for actions taken. Circumstances arising from teacher agreements, student and parent attitudes, district policy, and community pressures operated in various ways to constrain individual school and school administrator autonomy. The more effective principals employed the administrative team and other advisory

19

groups to protect and enlarge local autonomy to make decisions, plan actions, and solve problems at the building level.

Problem Solving, Planning, and Decision-Making Practices

All administrative team members that we observed had functional roles and represented their delegated areas of responsibility. The principal faced the task of developing a genuine team effort. In observing team and advisory group meetings, and in group and individual interviews, the site visitors found ample evidence of conflicts of interest, strong individual differences over policies and actions, and serious concerns about conditions in the schools. Those principals judged to be most effective met and resolved issues, as best they could, through the processes and procedures established for planning, decision making, and problem solving. They did other things, both tangible and intangible, some of which will be noted in this report. The quality of planning, decision making, and problem solving, however, and the administrative team's part in it, were clearly essential to the principal's success and to school productivity and satisfaction.

In every school visited, we found that the principal and the school had recently faced extremely difficult problems and/or conditions. These included racial tensions, suicides, drug abuse, large budget cuts and/or declining enrollments, imposed changes in graduation requirements, and violence and vandalism. In almost every case, schools addressed these problems and conditions while raising test scores, making improvements in curriculum and instruction, increasing parental involvement, and engaging in developmental projects. The administrative team under the leadership of the principal was the arena for planning, decision making, and problem solving.

Several conclusions can be drawn from the success stories documented during the site visits.

Problem Solving:

1. Principals established the administrative team as the final, formal structure for processing plans and decisions at the school site. Principals retained the final vote in this group.

2. Definite advisory bodies were created, including department and faculty advisory committees, student councils, and parent advisory boards. Written procedures were established to enable these groups to bring advice and to voice concerns to the team.

3. Clear, written procedures were published for bringing problems and proposals forward. Everyone knew how to influence a decision.

4. Every advisory group was open to any member of that group. Anyone desiring it could make a proposal to the appropriate advisory group and, if needed, to the administrative team.

5. Most advisory groups generated solutions before problems went to the administrative team for formal action.

Planning:

1. A planning process existed, beginning with individual teachers and staff members, for developing a department plan, and finally a school plan.

2. No plan was rejected for which funds were available and staff commitment was established, unless it clearly contradicted district policy or public law. A proposal, once approved, was fully supported by the administration.

3. Department and school plans included a goal and/or purpose statement, actions and activities, timelines, and cost estimates. Current-year plans at each level were evaluated as one basis for the next year's plan.

Decision Making:

1. Assistant principals and department chairs had full authority to make decisions within their written areas of authority.

2. Principals were decisive in making and/or approving decisions so that delays were avoided.

3. Principals followed up decisions and required reports to the administrative team, including projects for which they personally were responsible.

4. Prompt, public notice of decisions was given to faculty, students, and parents in bulletins and newsletters, as well as in presentations to appropriate groups.

The more effective principals in our sample were both open and decisive, although they did represent differing leadership styles. The observers of one principal wrote, "He is careful in considering ramifications of a problem, yet enough of a risk taker to take chances on others; egalitarian in approach to a wide variety of programs and personnel, yet astute enough to retain control of the deciding vote." Of another principal, a different pair of observers wrote, "Attention to detail is apparent from the job descriptions of assistant principals and department chairs, to the outlining of routines, to the descriptions of actions taken. This principal delegates within clearly defined limits while retaining ultimate authority and responsibility. There is dialog about every issue that departs from these defined limits, but decisions are made swiftly and actions are taken promptly. As the principal said, 'I tell everyone that bad news, unlike wine, does not improve with age'."

The case studies prepared for this report support the conclusion that effective principals develop strong, collaborative teams linked to advisory   21 *groups*. The primary advisory groups are faculty committees, department chairpersons, student councils, and parent advisory boards.

Variations Among Schools: Four Underlying Factors

Every school in our sample confronted unique internal and external conditions. Two schools in affluent neighborhoods of large cities, for example, were similar in size and staffing patterns, but had little in common in the circumstances affecting them. The first had a benevolent, decentralized district organization; the second, a tightly controlled and bureaucratic one. The first had a unified, supportive, and stable neighborhood; the second, a divided, contentious, and unstable one. The first had a satisfied and highly productive faculty; the second, an unsatisfied faculty of average productivity (based upon our instruments). The first had active, supportive, and highly achieving students; the second, troubled and perplexed though achieving students. The remaining schools in the sample showed similar internal and external differences.

Principals who really assumed responsibility set an agenda for the school, acted decisively to solve problems and improve conditions, and moved their schools ahead. These principals recognized that the principalship was a collegial responsibility, with authority delegated according to function, but with a team approach to the total school operation. Management functions were delegated as well as the required authority.

A primary function of the administrative team was the *coordination* of efforts for problem solving, planning, and decision making. This entailed data gathering and information sharing on the internal and external conditions affecting the school, with sufficient participation by advisory groups to ensure genuine understanding of problems and opportunities and commitment to solutions and interventions.

Variations existed among the schools on several conditions affecting administrative team performance; e.g., school size, the leadership style and individual proficiencies of principals, the severity of the problems faced, and availability of resources to deal with them. Four underlying factors emerged in team success in confronting these conditions. We will treat these as tentative hypotheses because of our limited sample, but the evidence strongly suggests that these four factors are significant to an understanding of the administrative team in schools.

1. *The most basic factor in team success is the degree of autonomy accorded the school by the district*, as reflected in district policies and regulations, teacher and employee agreements, and established practice. We encountered instances of disruption in school operations where a certain amount of latitude or procedures for granting exceptions would have permitted easier resolution of problems or innovative treatment. Restrictions occurred in many areas, including curriculum, attendance, personnel assignments, building use and

maintenance, purchasing, and reallocation of the in-school budget. Undue restrictions hampered and discouraged team efforts and wasted the time and energy of the principal.

2. *Position power of the principal within the school is a significant factor in team operation.* By position power we mean the amount of prestige a principal is accorded and has earned that facilitates the exercise of leadership. We have noted that some principals developed, or were accorded, a "zone of tolerance" for actions taken. Several of these principals used the administrative team to establish a common direction in meeting problems, to "buffer" themselves from minor disruptions and administrative details, and to actively support solutions. Delegated authority was one means of doing this.

   Earned influence derives from expectations set and realized by the principal and the members of the administrative team. These expectations and their realization must be created among faculty, students, and parents. Effective principals established clear problem-solving and decision-making procedures, exercised open communication and channeled it through appropriate procedures, and encouraged proposals. A "window of opportunity" may exist, especially for new principals, to set expectations, assume control, and be able to act decisively. In any event, a principal's capability and will to lead must be established and maintained. The position power of the principal conditions the capacity of the administrative team, either to act expeditiously on issues, problems, and opportunities or to become immersed in conflict and to be ineffective.

3. *The school-community environment with its values, expectations, and problems create a climate for the school apart from other influences.* One school-community clearly did not value academic excellence and only with extraordinary effort could the school reward and recognize achievement. Another school had difficulty getting the cooperation of community agencies to respond to serious security and drug problems. Others struggled with divided parent groups that fought over discipline rules, minimum dress requirements, grading practices, and attendance policies.

   The number of serious problems facing the schools in this study has already been mentioned. Schools inherited these conditions from their clientele, and the impact upon the school could not be avoided. The problems could not be handed to the district because the nature of the accommodations demanded solution at the school site. Teachers and support staff, if they are to fulfill their roles, cannot devote significant amounts of time and energy to these conditions. Nor can principals merely delegate housekeeping functions to assistant principals or other administrative staff and tackle the problems alone (establish policies that will be supported, create

23

and maintain communication links, build appropriate support structures, etc.). Our experience in examining this factor convinced us that the principalship, at least in larger schools, has grown too large for most individuals to manage efficiently. Even a team has trouble at times.

4. *The quality of staff members, characterized by their competence, diversity, and stability, is a factor in school productivity.* We did not set out initially to assess this dimension in the schools, but its importance became clear from an examination of all the case studies taken together. The cases contain rich evidence that can be illustrated by a few verbatim examples:

● "The accommodation of diverse student types and needs is a hallmark at (school). The entire student spectrum is addressed, from Advanced Placement and gifted programs to vocational and industrial arts, distributive education, and community-based instruction for the handicapped. There is widespread acceptance, and pride in this feeling of family tolerances for differences and diversity . . . This is possible because of the diversity of faculty background and the conscious efforts of the principal." (Investigator)

● "One A.P., in her development plan, undertook training in suicide prevention and gave inservice training to the faculty. Without warning, a suicide occurred, and we were ready. Now she has provided inservice throughout the district. Most faculty search for training opportunities, reading, critical thinking, values clarification, etc. and bring this expertise back to share with us." (Principal)

● "Certain faculty are part of the informal leadership structure. They have been teaching a long time. . . . Dr. (name) respects and admires them. They make the school look good." (Investigator)

● "Chairs and teachers have insight into problems. They have taken initiatives in tardiness, adding A.P. classes, moving activities out of the school day, and in acquiring needed funds and equipment where funds are not available." (Assistant Principal)

● "We have access to anyone, teachers or administrators, and they almost always can tell us what we want to know or get what we need . . . . They react quickly and they know what they are doing . . . . This is a competent faculty and an able group of administrators." (Parent group)

● "The teachers here love to teach and they are good. My counselor put a lot of pressure on me to go to college. She showed me what I needed to do. I did it, and I'm going. . . . The principal really listens to us, and he pushes every reasonable project we plan and presents it to the administrative advisory committee." (Student group)

Role of the Principal

24   Creating conditions that permit a school to survive and prosper in

terms of the four underlying factors noted above moved principals to some interesting and creative approaches. We can offer several illustrations of administrative ingenuity from our case data.

1. Principals, working with the administrative team, set the agenda for their schools. They created advisory groups using formal procedures to get input from faculty, parents, and students. They built coalitions and, through these groups, generated support for decisions made by the administrative team.

2. Principals created a positive image for their schools. In two of the schools visited, part of each team meeting was devoted to the "good news." Note was made of any individual (student, teacher, parent) who had achieved something helpful to the school's image. Individual achievements as well as school activities and programs were announced in school, released to the press, and summarized in a special section of the parent newsletter. Calls and letters were regularly sent to parents about their student's achievements.

3. Principals aggressively pursued autonomy for themselves and the school. In one school, many changes were made with the help of advisory groups and the administrative team, some without specific district sanction. This principal said, "We are here to solve problems. We go ahead, even publish it, and then back off if we have to." In another school, an interview with a group of teachers established the general consensus that "He (principal) treats us like professionals. We have a great deal of autonomy in our day-to-day work, but his is the final word on major changes."

4. Principals were able to delegate authority at all levels but especially within the administrative team. In the most productive schools, detailed job descriptions and organizational charts were available and used. As one assistant principal reported, "The principal told me once, over a matter I clearly should have handled but sent on to him, if you can't do your job, I don't need you." In another school, the principal required an assistant principal to file charges against a teacher judged by the A.P to be unsatisfactory. In this same school, the administrative team held an annual retreat to review job descriptions and performance.

5. Principals in productive schools expended much effort with the administrative team to bring innovative projects to the school and to discover training opportunities for teachers and staff. They found creative ways to raise funds for resources and travel from student activities, local foundations, and service clubs.

6. Principals in productive schools were sensitive to issues and problems and could anticipate how they might affect their schools and what might be the consequences. Issues were targeted and specific

approaches planned. Principals anticipated increased graduation requirements, changes in the composition of a school's student population, budget reductions, and declining enrollments. Plans were formulated and in some cases changes already made before the district had taken the item under consideration.

7. A few principals staffed key roles to achieve diversity in their schools by what is known in dramatic circles as "casting against type." Persons of differing views were deliberately included to provide a range of opinion and to create a team capable of interacting with differing constituencies.

In every productive school, the principal was the central person. The administrative team members specialized in their areas of competence but shared the total responsibility for the school. There was much informal contact among team members, but they met, deliberated, and made decisions within a formal structure established by the principal. The team under the principal was the final body to which other groups reported. Plans, problem solutions, and decisions were made final in team meetings; responsibilities were assigned, and actions coordinated. If team members had authority commensurate with their responsibilities and were unified in support of actions taken, positive results invariably resulted. Even schools facing overwhelming difficulties were productive and satisfying places for faculty to work and students to study.

IV Instructional Leadership

The second major research question addressed in the study was, "What is the administrative team's view of instructional leadership and how is it operationalized?" This important question acknowledges that the principal's job focus has recently been redirected from school management to instructional leadership (Johnson and Snyder, 1986). In fact, the main body of effective schools' research and educational leadership literature has repeatedly emphasized the importance of instructional leadership in school improvement and indicated certain essential behaviors that must be exercised by school leaders. These include: (a) identification and expression of a set of values and expectations that place a high priority on instruction in the total school program; (b) a clear instructional goal focus with systematic plans for accomplishment; (c) the ability of principals to share instructional leadership functions with others; and (d) maintenance of a safe and orderly school environment that promotes learning and protects students' instructional time (Bird and Little, 1985; Dwyer et al., 1983; Glatthorn and Newberg, 1984; Keefe, 1987; Murphy et al., 1982; and Persell, Crookston, and Lyons, 1982).

The researchers interviewed school leaders at each of the eight sites to determine how the administrative team understood and provided instructional leadership. The interview protocols incorporated a series of questions, prompts, and probes designed to encourage specific answers. Interviewees were asked, for example, to describe one of their major accomplishments in the school. If no particular accomplishment surfaced, they were asked to discuss some positive change that had taken place in the school. Additional questions helped the researchers to gain a clearer understanding of the goals, motives, and procedures surrounding the event. These questions included: "Why did you select this accomplishment?"; "Why do you consider it a success?"; "How much did it cost?"; and "How did you get the resources to achieve this success?" If the program described did not involve curriculum or instruction, administrators were asked to relate a specific success in these areas.

If respondents' success stories were unrelated to the instructional program, this gave some indication of the priority placed on instruction in the school. Follow-up probes and cues elicited information about a range of instructional leadership behaviors such as resource procurement and allocation, program evaluation, and so forth. These inquiries produced a considerable amount of evidence that was sifted by the researchers for insight into the complicated process of instructional leadership.

This chapter reports findings on the nature of instructional leadership and how it is exercised in schools. The findings probe instructional leadership from multiple perspectives—as seen by administrators, teachers, and students.

What Instructional Leadership Is Not

Traditionally, the principal has been regarded as the instructional leader in a school. Principals have usually not had to earn this mantle; it has more or less gone with the territory. Few persons in or out of the educational community seem to have a clear understanding of the meaning of instructional leadership. This uncertainty perhaps has contributed to the notion that many principals are functional instructional leaders.

Most principals who took part in this study believed that they were instructional leaders, but the view was not always shared by those around them. When principals were asked to define "instructional leadership," their responses were as varied as the situations in which their leadership was exercised. Two definitions suggested by principals in vastly different settings will serve to illustrate this diversity of opinion. The first principal was very precise in his definition:

> Instructional leadership can be categorized under four components: (1) Knowing the program (curriculum); (2) Being aware of the positive and negative effects of the program on students; (3) Knowing which programs can be changed and which cannot; and (4) Being involved in changing programs and influencing others to do so.

A second principal expressed a more global perspective:

> Instruction is the most important thing in the school. All that we do in this school is done to support instruction. Any new programs that we implement, purchases we make, disciplinary actions, or even field trips students take, are all done in the interest of improving instruction. Instructional leadership is setting the correct tone and promoting an atmosphere so that teachers can teach and students can learn. Everything else (related to instruction) falls under atmosphere.

It may be difficult, even for those actively engaged in the process, to characterize the essence of instructional leadership, but it is decidedly easier to describe what instructional leadership is *not*. Instructional leadership is most certainly not a discrete set of behaviors or activities such as ordering curriculum materials, monitoring and evaluating teachers, or even providing staff development. Any or all of these behaviors may be directly related to instructional leadership, but, in isolation, the specific behaviors are not synonymous with the role.

The principal of one visitation site was very adept at planning, organizing, and generally getting tasks done. He was very knowledgeable about instruction and could discuss concepts such as time-on-task and academic learning time with authority. This principal, whom we shall call Mr. Young, was particularly effective managing the budget in support of the academic program and could cite numerous examples of instructional innovations introduced during his tenure. For example, he had strengthened the role of department chairpersons by including them in all major decisions about the instructional program. He had initiated an awards program to recognize students for academic success and an Advanced Placement program in the physical sciences. Nonetheless, faculty members did not see him or the administration as the chief source of instructional leadership. Indeed, most teachers thought that instructional leadership was totally lacking in the school.

Somehow, Mr. Young had failed to communicate to the faculty and students his commitment to the importance of the instructional program. He had plans and goals, but teachers and students felt excluded from his vision. Mr. Young stated during an interview that academic excellence was his primary goal for the next few years. When asked how this goal would be measured, he pointed to a general increase in the school's standardized test scores and an increase (up to 50 percent) in the proportion of graduates going to four-year colleges.

Mr. Young had clearly been successful in bringing about needed changes in the school's instructional program, and he could formulate, at least in general terms, some intermediate goals for the school, but the teachers freely voiced their frustrations about an apparent lack of direction. They were unanimous in their desire for a "sense of direction" and some "common goals" to guide the institution. As one senior faculty member expressed it:

> There is no commitment to excellence, no vision for the future. There is no plan to make us the best at anything. We don't know if we are trying to be the best in the state, the best in the country, or the best this side of the river. Whatever is, seems to be good enough.

Despite a number of successful innovations in this school, the general quality of the academic programs (as measured by standardized tests) had declined. The teaching staff was regarded as excellent by everyone we interviewed, but few teachers were willing to invest extra time and energy to work with students outside class. Enthusiasm, excitement, and commitment were lacking. A veteran teacher recalled the "good old days:"

> There was a day when teachers would stay after school and help the children; talk to one another about their hopes for tomorrow. Why, many of them would be here until five o'clock. Now, comes 3:15, they're gone. If children need help, they can come back tomorrow.
> Today, the things we dwell on are the failures, the negative things.

Although Mr. Young displayed some of the behaviors and successfully carried out many of the activities associated with instructional leadership, he was not recognized as an instructional leader by his faculty.

29

Instructional leadership clearly is more than a discrete set of activities and behaviors.

Some principals in this study saw instructional leadership primarily as an attitude. These principals regarded themselves as instructional leaders simply because they advocated the preeminence of the instructional program. They took advantage of every opportunity to remind students, teachers, parents, and the community at large that the primary purpose of the school was to promote student learning and that everyone must dedicate his or her efforts to this purpose. Several principals freely admitted that this was their primary, if not only, responsibility as the instructional leader of the school.

Principals who practiced this form of instructional leadership saw themselves as distant resources. One remarked, "my job is to model, to demonstrate an interest in helping teachers the way I expect teachers to help students." The desired objective in demonstrating a caring attitude toward teachers was for teachers to demonstrate a caring attitude toward students. One principal described it as, "a crusading mentality, an abiding stock of good intentions that go beyond the end of the school day, and beyond the fence that encircles the campus buildings." These principals felt that their main instructional responsibility was to develop an instructional climate conducive to good teaching: adequate materials, a stable environment, good student discipline, and a general attitude supportive of instruction. This view was summed up by several principals who constantly reminded themselves to "keep out of the way of good teachers who were doing their jobs."

To the contrary, instructional leadership is more than a philosophical bias, a written mission statement, or rhetoric about the importance of instruction in a particular school. Instructional leadership is more than an attitude. Cheerleading, per se, will do little to raise the academic outcomes of a school, and may, in fact, inhibit progress if teachers are given unconditional freedom in determining content and teaching methodology.

One of the schools in the study had experienced steadily declining academic outcomes for several years, as measured by standardized test scores. Yet this school's principal—we will call him Dr. Good—was highly regarded by both his peers and constituents as a successful instructional leader. In reality, Dr. Good was an extremely effective cheerleader. He was repeatedly described by teachers and others as "the most positive person we've ever met." One teacher even characterized him as "the best cheerleader we have." Very little direct supervision or academic coordination existed in the school. Some major academic programs had no standard curriculum, and teachers were free to teach whatever they felt was appropriate in the ways they felt it should be taught. All the while, Dr. Good was reminding teachers to "plow to the end of the row," and that there were "no goof-off days in the calendar."

Some very good things were certainly happening in Dr. Good's school. He had successfully created a warm and accepting atmosphere for students, teachers, parents, and citizens in the face of district upheavals that directly affected the school. He had established and maintained programs appropriate for all students in the school. He was notably successful in garnering additional resources during a period of tight fiscal constraints. But in the final analysis, these measures had not raised test scores nor even stabilized them. His expectations and actions had not convinced people that instruction was the most important thing in the school. *Instructional leadership is more than just an attitude.*

What Is Instructional Leadership?

If instructional leadership is not just a set of discrete activities and behaviors, nor simply an attitude, then what is it? Our observations of and discussions with administrators and teachers would lead us to define instructional leadership as the initiation and implementation of planned changes in a school's instructional program, through the influence and direction of the various constituencies in the school. NASSP's *Instructional Leadership Handbook* (Keefe and Jenkins, 1984; 1990) calls it "the principal's role in providing direction, resources and support to teachers and students for the improvement of teaching and learning in the school." Instructional leadership begins with an attitude, an expressed commitment to student productivity, from which emanates values, behaviors, and functions deliberately designed to foster, facilitate, and support student satisfaction and achievement.

The following sections explore some of the most important characteristics of instructional leadership observed by study team members during the school visits.

Instructional leadership is a shared responsibility. As such, it is not vested in a single person or role category in the school. Instructional leadership is not limited to the school administration. In no instance did we find a school in which the principal was the single source of instructional leadership; only in a few instances was the principal even characterized as the primary source. Assistant principals, and more often, department chairpersons were identified as major sources of instructional leadership in particular schools. We also found that district-level consultants as well as teachers were frequently credited with providing significant instructional leadership. The most common pattern was shared instructional leadership, with the administrative team (principals and assistants) providing support to department chairpersons who exercised functional leadership by working with faculty members in various departments. The department chairpersons were frequently assisted by district supervisors or consultants.

Instructional leadership, then, is not solely an administrative function. The most common source of practical instructional leadership is the

31

department chairperson. Chairs typically are responsible for, and work fairly closely with, three to eight teachers who teach the same subject. Most instructional concerns are addressed at department meetings. General staff meetings on instructional issues are rare, perhaps only two or three times a semester, and even then, specific instructional planning is seldom discussed. Departmental meetings, on the other hand, are held frequently and often deal with particular instructional problems. A member of the management team may be present at department meetings, but department heads usually provide the direct assistance and guidance to teachers.

In most instances, teachers told us that they "never sought the advice of the principal in instructional matters" and that discussion of instructional improvement tended to be department-centered rather than school-centered. When instructional issues occasionally turned up on faculty meeting agendas, contrary to what might be expected, principals rarely emphasized teachers' responsibility for student achievement. As one teacher remarked, "Our principal understands that grades and test scores are not all the teacher's fault."

Given the complex nature of the American secondary school, it is not surprising that a pattern of shared instructional leadership exists. Instructional programs in high schools are both diverse and extensive, with many content areas and sections ranging from remedial to Advanced Placement. Most programs are highly content-centered, requiring supervision from individuals with technical competence beyond the range of most principals. Schools also have responsibility for many other important functions such as transportation, discipline, social growth, and psychological and career counseling. All these functions take time to manage, and invariably require the daily attention of principals and assistant principals.

Without exception, all the principals in the study felt a strong obligation to provide significant instructional leadership in their schools. The reality in most situations, however, was that principals lacked the time (or did not schedule it) for the things they thought they should do. Most expressed frustration that the managerial aspects of their job tugged at them and legitimately pulled them away many times from instructional leadership responsibilities. This frustration was mirrored in the comments of one principal who, when asked if he considered himself to be an instructional leader, replied:

> In this state, a principal can't be an instructional leader. Most principals are managers rather than instructional leaders. I guess I'm a combination of manager and instructional leader; but I think I could be an instructional leader in a larger school.

The high level of frustration expressed by principals in this area was consistent with data reported in Volume I of this study. The national sample of principals (1988) reported that "time taken up by administrative detail" and a general "lack of time" were the chief roadblocks to their jobs. In the national survey, principals ranked program development as their number one priority—how they should spend their time—but admitted that program had to take a back seat to more immediate problems. The time required to administer complex academic programs coupled with the content and technical expertise needed to supervise them effectively dictates that instructional leadership be a shared function in most high schools.

Instructional leadership is situational. Instructional leadership is perhaps not much different from other kinds of leadership. It requires vision, flexibility, and common sense. Successful administrators know that an ideal faculty needs a spectrum of experience. The absence of a significant role type can seriously undermine the entire ensemble. Different skills are needed in different situations. Instructional success often hinges on a person's strengths in defined areas at a particular time in a specific place under a precise set of circumstances.

In districts where curriculum development is centralized, where there are excellent teachers and competent department chairpersons, and where students are successful and motivated, the principal's instructional leadership will be more supportive than directive. This principal can direct his or her energy to other facets of the school program while providing resources for the instructional staff.

In a different situation, where a school has bottomed out academically, instructional leadership may require a completely different approach. When students do not achieve and some teachers have given up, while others simply do not care, it may be necessary for the administrative team to supervise teachers very closely. It may even be necessary to bypass department chairpersons to force a measure of quality control on classrooms. The principal may have to set expectations for student and teacher performance quite deliberately and enforce these expectations when they are not met. The administrative team may have to initiate changes in academic programs even without the cooperation of some staff members. Instructional leadership in such an ineffective school may need to be extremely directive rather than supportive.

A particular approach to instructional leadership must be evaluated in the light of its effectiveness in a given situation. Whether highly supportive or highly directive, it cannot be judged ineffective simply because it goes against the grain of conventional wisdom. Supportive leadership should not be disdained, for example, simply because of the recent emphasis on forceful leadership, while directive leadership should not be discounted because it sometimes runs counter to democratic ideals. The situation governs the call. Any successful instructional environment has a systematic network tying together the principal, assistant principals, department heads, and teachers. In some situations, instructional leadership only calls for modeling and supportive interpersonal relations. In other situations, the connections must be established quite deliberately.

Instructional leadership is planned. Successful leaders know that progress is somehow tied to positive changes in an organization. Planning is discussed in some detail in Chapter III, but it is important to reaffirm here that our school visits reinforced our previously held convictions. When no planning exists, no positive changes occur. When no organized plan is present, no comprehensive strategies will exist, especially not in written form. This is true for the instructional program as well as for other aspects of the school.

The study team witnessed a wide disparity in the quality of planning for instructional improvement, ranging from total absence to intricate commit-tee structures for identifying needs and interventions. The most sophisti-cated example of instructional planning in the study reflected a long-range plan in place for five years. The plan was updated yearly with input from teachers, students, and parents. School plans were developed from the bottom up. Objectives were initiated by teachers in the departments. These went to the administrative council where school-level objectives were formulated for discussion in faculty, student council, and parent advisory meetings. With input from these sources, objectives were modified as necessary and sent to the district office.

At the time of our site visit to this school, six study groups were already examining problem areas in curriculum, homework, study skills, classroom management, administrative burdens on teachers, and grading practices. Planning did not stop with policy recommendations, but focused on specific corrective measures. Each department established objectives keyed to the total school plan and each teacher developed three or four similar objectives to be accomplished during the year.

Generally, however, planning for instructional improvement was sadly lacking in most of the schools visited. Neither diagnostic assessment, standardized achievement testing, nor formal program evaluation were evident in most schools in ways that could inform systematic planning or decision making. There was little indication of organized planning. No comprehensive strategies for planned change existed, at least not in written form. Many of the administrators simply felt that they were too busy with more immediate concerns. Informal is the only word that could accurately describe the kind of planning we observed in most places. This laissez faire attitude may be one outcome of a heavy district emphasis on centralization. Perhaps too much reliance is being placed on district-level intervention and direction. Even school inservice programs were planned at the district level.

Instructional leadership is enhanced by a common purpose. Regardless of the situation in which instructional leadership is exercised, how directive or how supportive the approach taken, or the manner in which leadership is shared, results will invariably be enhanced if a common purpose is evident in a school. Principals, teachers, students, and parents were asked in each school about the primary purposes of schooling. Most stated their views in a few words. Schools with evidence of effective instructional leadership (rising test scores, risk-taking behavior, shared responsibility, and so forth), exhibited general agreement among all segments about the primary purposes of schooling.

The following statements represent some of the most universally held beliefs about the primary purposes of schooling in the schools visited.

- The purpose of schooling is to serve the needs of students instructionally, socially, in all ways; to help students fit in and excel.
- The primary purpose of the school is to take each student to his or her ultimate capabilities.
- The school's primary responsibility is to provide each individual with the opportunity to develop the skills necessary for living in an ever-changing environment as a positive and productive member of society.

In every instance, regardless of whether the school was considered more or less effective, regardless of the manner in which instructional leadership was shared, regardless of the directness or indirectness of the particular approach used, the primary purposes of schooling were invariably *student-centered*. How a shared common purpose affected instructional leadership in a particular situation hinged not on the purposes themselves, but on the level of awareness and acceptance of the purposes by those in the school. Schools in which the primary purposes were constantly showcased seemed to enjoy more harmonious and supportive working relationships among staff, students, and community. A willingness existed in such schools to sacrifice and exert greater effort to improve instructional opportunities for students. Shared purpose seems to be prerequisite to mutual trust and respect.

Instructional leadership helps break down barriers to create an atmosphere of mutual respect and trust. Schools are social institutions, but people in schools tend to be isolated from one another. Students are isolated from teachers who in turn are isolated from other teachers and from administrators. Instructional leaders understand that positive change occurs when people have opportunities to come together, to share problems, and to seek common solutions.

Several of the principals we studied were very adept at breaking down barriers between factions in their schools. One principal in particular devoted tremendous energy to bringing all the people in his school together. Almost all his time was spent away from his office. He not only visited classrooms, but participated in class discussions as if he were a student, asking and responding to questions. Students and teachers alike acknowledged that this principal, Mr. Friendly, spent time in most of the classrooms each day, constantly encouraging teachers to "serve the needs of the students." We were told that Mr. Friendly never left a teacher's classroom

35

without some positive comment about the lesson. He could call most students by name and students felt comfortable in approaching him with their concerns. Because of his visibility in the school, Friendly was identified universally as "the instructional leader."

Principal Friendly had gone beyond the so-called "open-door" approach to school administration to something that might better be described as the "open-principal" approach. He was everywhere, in classrooms, the cafeteria, the student parking lot, visible proof of "management by wandering around." He went to great lengths to inspire participation in school life by encouraging massive input from students, parents, and teachers. In Mr. Friendly's view, "such an approach gives everyone ownership in the school and creates an atmosphere where all of us who have an interest in the school can win together."

Friendly could almost be described as paternal in his dealings with the day-to-day problems of the school family. He was universally perceived as a genuinely interested and caring person. His advice and assistance were frequently solicited by students, teachers, parents, and even his fellow principals. On several occasions during the site visit, Friendly received telephone calls from other principals in the district who wanted his thoughts on programs they were contemplating for their schools, or they simply wanted to "run a problem by him." Mr. Friendly's decisions were almost always accepted without argument. Students and staff members readily admitted, "I don't always get what I want," but they all seemed to agree, "I always feel that my opinions are appreciated and respected."

Friendly was not the only principal who recognized the need to break down barriers between the various groups of people who make up a school. Other principals did most of the things he did to a lesser degree, as well as employ other strategies to bring people together and make them aware of the needs and accomplishments of others. An elaborate committee structure was an approach favored by several of the principals studied. Recognition and awards programs were popular with some principals, as well as public announcements, bulletin boards, and newsletters. Good human relations aside, however, perhaps the most important consequence of an atmosphere of mutual respect and trust in a school setting is another element of instructional leadership, an environment for risk taking.

Instructional leadership involves risk taking. In all the schools visited, whenever the study team saw good instructional programs, almost always an element of risk was involved. It seemed that risk was directly related to positive growth. The more risks, the bigger the risks, the more people involved in risk-taking behavior, the better the outcomes.

Why risk-taking behavior should be associated with instructional leadership is not absolutely clear. Perhaps it has something to do with the bureaucratic nature of schools (or, more precisely, school districts). Several of the principals lamented the difficulty of getting authorization for needed changes through the grinding bureaucracy of their district hierarchy and how inflexible and resistant to change top-level managers seemed to be. Principals were frustrated with their inability to deal expeditiously with problems that many times were unique to their schools. They were forced to "go through the channels." In some instances, the more successful principals bypassed the red tape or acted pending approval. This approach seemed to motivate others. At the very least, it was noticed and appreciated within the school.

In one school, the management team actively encouraged problem identification and resolution. The administration strongly encouraged groups and individuals to try out ideas rather than just talk about them. The principal noted with pride that "when an idea comes up or a suggestion is made that gets support, we go all out for it." No plan for improvement was turned down if it had funding and staff commitment.

Many changes were implemented in this particular school without district permission, and in some cases, even without district notification. The principal's style was to act first and repent later. "We go ahead, even publish it (a planned change), and then back off if we have to." Teachers, assistant principals, coordinators, and students all mentioned this gambling attitude and cited a number of specific examples of innovation without prior sanction. Some of these innovations included combining two courses in the curriculum, a new writing project, a school tardy policy, resolution of the smoking issue, a suicide prevention program, a tutoring project, and a distinguished scholars program. None of these projects were cleared with the district prior to implementation and some were even counter to established policy. Interestingly, several of the programs have now been adopted districtwide.

In another school, the principal had consistently demonstrated his willingness to take risks, to trust his best judgment as well as that of others. He had a reputation for doing what was best for the school even if forced to deviate from established district policy. Students related instances where the principal had allowed them to do something out of the ordinary because "he trusted our ability to bring it off." One example involved an ill-fated "toga day" when students were allowed to come to school dressed in Roman costumes. The event backfired, and the principal willingly took the blame from the community and the district administration. The students seemed to be genuinely sorry they had let their school down.

Perhaps the most important thing to stress here is that risks were always undertaken for a definite reason. Instructional leaders take risks, not because they are foolhardy or careless, but because they know the effect of risk-taking behavior on others. They carefully consider both the desirable and undesirable consequences of their actions and make informed decisions to encourage their colleagues to take similar risks.

When instructional leadership was present in a school to a significant degree, a high tolerance for risk was also in evidence. Instructional leaders simply refused to let red tape strangle innovation. Risktakers were even creatively insubordinate on certain occasions. Few who really knew them, however, questioned their motives for swimming against the current.

Instructional leadership is characterized by informed behaviors. Earlier in this chapter, we asserted that instructional leadership was not simply a collection of attitudes nor a set of discrete behaviors, but involved the integration of both attitudes and behaviors. Leadership is manifested as informed behaviors, or "attitudes in action," on the part of instructional leaders. Instructional leaders do not engage in behaviors simply because they are included in a job description or an evaluation checklist. Instead, they behave in certain ways because they know that these behaviors are likely to have a positive effect on teachers or students, and ultimately a positive impact on the instructional program. The activities of instructional leaders are goal-directed in this sense; they are performed with a final result in mind, the improvement of the instructional program.

Visiting classrooms or observing teachers at work, for example, has limited value in itself. Some principals and other instructional leaders are convinced that if they make the rounds of the classrooms from time to time, sit in the back of the room with arms folded while smiling and nodding their heads, and then give teachers a friendly slap on the back, they are effectively functioning as instructional leaders. We saw this kind of instructional leadership in some of the schools we visited. In most instances, however, principals became involved only when instructional problems arose.

There is undeniable excitement in the simple act of watching some teachers at work, but the real payoff comes, not in the act of observing, but in what results. Follow-up conferences with teachers, sharing improvement strategies to sharpen teaching skills, and breaking down barriers between teachers and administrators, and between teachers and teachers—these are the valuable outcomes of teacher observation. Observation must be linked with specific instructional behaviors. These behaviors do not occur in isolation. They are performed in sets, for particular reasons, with definite ends in mind. When leader behavior and attitudes are informed, meaningful instructional leadership can take place.

What Is the Essential Nature of the Instructional Leader?

Thus far in this chapter we have discussed the concept of instructional leadership in terms of what it is and what it is not. But what makes instructional leaders different from others? How can someone become more effective in meeting his or her responsibilities as an instructional leader? These are difficult questions and, based on the data from our field studies, probably unanswerable in a definitive form. We can make a few valid inferences from what we observed, however, and attempt to shed some light on a difficult subject.

A brief summary of the previous discussion may be an appropriate place to begin. We have said that instructional leadership is not a discrete set of behaviors, and that it is not simply a collection of attitudes. We have also said that instructional leadership is not vested in a single job title or individual; almost anyone—principal, assistant principal, teacher, counselor, librarian, consultant—may function as an instructional leader in a particular school. We have further taken the position that instructional leadership is like other forms of leadership in that it is situational. It depends on a variety of conditions that may or may not be present in individual school settings. Instructional leadership is planned rather than random, enhanced by a shared common purpose, acts to break down barriers between people and to promote mutual respect and trust, and involves an element of risk taking. Finally, we have described the practice of instructional leadership in terms of informed behaviors or attitudes that are almost always planned in the sense that they are goal-directed.

All the elements of instructional leadership discussed in this chapter could easily be reduced to a short paragraph. It would be easy to say that an instructional leader is any person in a school who assumes a responsibility for the improvement of the instructional program. The instructional leader knows how to plan, and recognizes the importance of fostering a positive climate in the school through shared purposes that break down barriers between people and promote mutual respect and trust. The instructional leader is a calculated risktaker who understands the impact of his/her actions on the behavior of groups and individuals in the school.

These behaviors most certainly characterize facets of instructional leadership and of the instructional leader, but they represent an incomplete characterization. So many other aspects of instructional leadership do not easily spring to mind, do not fit neatly into the flow of the narrative, or simply defy description in conventional terms. Realizing this, we will try to list several other qualities that we observed in principals who clearly were instructional leaders.

Instructional leaders know what they believe. One burden of instructional leadership is that the leader must make countless decisions about what goals to pursue, how they will be pursued, and how much of the available resources will be dedicated to reaching them. There are many groups and individuals who seek to influence educational decisions to suit their own interests. Unless the instructional leader has a firmly established and integrated set of beliefs to guide decisions, he or she will be unduly influenced by advocates of narrow special interests. An instructional leader who has no absolutes, no inviolable ideals, will be judged by others as inconsistent and untrustworthy, and will ultimately be unable to lead. Instructional leaders must work hard to stay abreast of issues and knowledge affecting students and schools, to form beliefs about these issues and facts, and to let these beliefs guide them in all their decisions.

Instructional leaders are aware of how important it is to start off right. A definable window of opportunity may exist for a new principal, or anyone accepting an instructional leadership role. While this window is open, the leader must act decisively. If existing ideas and practices go unchallenged for a period of time, the leader will surely meet much stronger opposition in trying to change them. As one principal told us, "If I could do one thing differently, I would be more assertive in the beginning. I realize now that I don't control some aspects of the school operation, and frankly, I don't know how I'm going to do so without a considerable upheaval and a lot of interpersonal conflict." Our observations in several settings led us to conclude that an instructional leader's will to lead must be established relatively early if he/she is to lead at all.

Instructional leaders always make decisions in the best interests of their primary clients. It is tempting from time to time for leaders to make a decision in the interest of someone other than students. For example, a teacher may want to teach a class for which he or she is not particularly well-suited, or a school board member may push hard for the employment of a less-qualified applicant for a position. Invariably, decisions that put the needs of others—teachers, board members, parents—ahead of the needs of students have an adverse effect on a school. Leaders who put the needs of others ahead of those of students will have their motives carefully scrutinized and ultimately fail as instructional leaders.

Instructional leaders do not ignore problems; they relentlessly seek them out and deal with them. Real problems never go away; they grow and grow until they become unmanageable, ultimately threatening the survival of someone or something that is important to the school. Instructional leaders are problem solvers. They understand that the function of leadership is to solve problems, not avoid them. They are constantly assessing situations, evaluating results, and actively seeking input from others about what can be changed or improved in some way.

Instructional leaders pay attention to the little things. Everyone does the big things. We did not observe a single school where the principal had not hired teachers to fill existing vacancies, ordered textbooks to start the year, or developed a master schedule. Carrying out the major job responsibilities in a school does not certify an instructional leader. Principals characterized as instructional leaders were noted for their attention to detail. They did the little things as well as the big ones. They encouraged students or teachers when they were down, or smiled in the face of adversity because they knew how important it was to radiate hope. Caring is reflected in the little things, so instructional leaders pay attention to them.

Instructional leaders earn their mantles. This discussion of instructional leadership began with an assertion that principals have long been regarded as *the* instructional leaders of their schools. Traditionally, this mantle of instructional leader was accorded principals because of their formal leadership role in schools. They did not have to earn the distinction; it came with the territory.

40

The primary job emphasis of principals has overtly shifted from school management to instructional leadership. The expectation that principals actually perform as instructional leaders now strongly influences how successful they are perceived to be. The title of principal is no longer a synonym for *the* instructional leader of the school. Instructional leadership can encompass any number of individuals in a school but the distinction will be recognized only when it is earned.

In the final analysis, there is no simple formula for success. Instructional leadership is manifested in many different forms depending on the circumstances in a school. Regardless of the form, however, or who exercises it, instructional leadership is likely to be the most important function in a school for creating a productive and satisfying environment.

V Satisfaction and Productivity

Students, parents, and other citizens share with educators three common expectations for schools. First of all, schools are expected to be effective organizations in which students achieve various outcomes judged to be desirable by society. Second, schools are expected to provide a positive environment that is a source of satisfaction for students and educators. And, finally, public schools are expected to be efficient (i.e., cost-effective) in using public resources to bring about these outcomes.

Expectations of satisfaction, effectiveness, and efficiency appear to be widespread in the United States, but agreement on the relative importance of these three goals varies. The efficiency of a school, in part, is influenced by a community's willingness to pay for educational opportunities. An effective school, one that is achieving excellence, may be either efficient or inefficient. School effectiveness, in turn, may be influenced by the level of available resources. (Caution should be exercised, however, in assuming that increases in expenditures will lead to improved effectiveness.) The highly complex relationships among satisfaction, effectiveness, and efficiency are illustrated in some of the basic and supplementary data collected for the eight high schools of this study (see Table 5.1).

The first volume of the study, *High School Leaders and Their Schools*, *Volume I*, (Pellicer et al., 1988) described the 1980s as "the decade of the principalship." The principalship was defined as "more than a single person or role position," affirming that an individual serving as principal and an administrative team were necessary to promote educational effectiveness in a school. How this team supports school excellence is one of the three major research questions in this second phase of the study, and the one addressed in this chapter. "How does the administrative team achieve optimum productivity and satisfaction?"

The eight schools described in Chapter I and profiled in Table 5.1 are generally representative of high schools in the United States. Their selection was made after a consideration of multiple sources of data. Intensive site visits were made to each school to collect additional information. The varied forms of data included surveys of teacher and student climate and satisfaction, measures of productivity, and analyses of efficiency. The collection and analyses of these data were undertaken with the Comprehensive Assessment of School Environments (CASE) battery developed by NASSP's Task Force on Effective School Climate. (The CASE Model is shown in Appendix B.)

TABLE 5.1
A Profile of Selected Schools and Measures of Satisfaction and Productivity

Data Category	School 01	School 02	School 03	School 04	School 05	School 06	School 07	School 08
Type of Community	Rural	Suburb	Urban	SMCITY	SMCITY	Rural	Urban	Urban
Years Principal in School	2–3	5–8	8+	5–8	8+	8+	8+	5–8
Sex of Principal	M	M	M	M	M	M	M	M
Ethnicity of Principal	W	W	B	B	W	W	W	W
Percentage of Students in Remedial Programs	20–29%	10–19%	10–19%	<10	10–19%	10–19%	<10%	<10%
Percentage of Students in Vocational Programs	<10%	20–29%	30–39%	40–49%	30–39%	40–49%	<10%	10–19%
Percentage of Students who Matriculate Postsecondary	60–69%	40–49%	70–79%	40–49%	50–59%	50–59%	80–89%	70–79%
Student Climate Score (39)*	36.4	43.0	40.1	40.8	47.0	45.1	38.5	43.9
Teacher Climate Score (43)*	36.3	42.4	37.7	45.4	49.7	44.3	42.1	46.5
Student Satisfaction Score (58)*	53.2	63.4	61.6	61.1	66.4	62.0	55.2	61.2
Teacher Satisfaction Score (29)*	22.8	27.2	27.3	29.8	35.4	29.3	25.7	31.5
Efficiency Rating	75%	89%	93%	NA	87%	84%	100%	81%
Math Score (50)*	18	65	24	NA	78	44	93	73
Math Contribution to Efficiency	0%	26%	0%	NA	42%	0%	4%	40%
Reading Score (50)*	34	58	24	NA	60	48	88	63
Reading Contribution to Efficiency	0%	0%	0%	NA	0%	0%	59%	0%
Student Self-Efficacy Score (2.14)*	1.88	2.07	2.16	NA	2.07	2.18	2.14	1.80
Student Self-Efficacy Score Contribution to Efficiency	75%	63%	93%	NA	45%	84%	38%	41%
Student Attendance	89%	90%	90%	NA	94%	93%	93%	93%
Per Pupil Expenditure (dollars)	3635	4380	2980	NA	3500	4292	3325	3079
Percentage *Not* Receiving Free or Reduced Lunch	91%	91%	78%	NA	100%	74%	99%	100%
Percentage Non-Minority Students	100%	98%	40%	NA	97%	99%	92%	80%
Percentage Stability in Student Population	85%	50%	84%	NA	97%	97%	73%	73%

*Total sample mean or median

During the site visits, focused interview questions helped to identify both formal and informal procedures used to define and measure school success (i.e., satisfaction and productivity). Other documentation was also collected such as local survey data, reports of student performance on standardized tests, and copies of self-studies and accreditation reports. These information sources suggested various explanations for the levels of satisfaction, productivity, and efficiency found in the eight schools.

Influence of School Climate

Climate reflects school culture. If a school has a positive climate, its cultural norms and expectations are positively perceived. Climate then is a good general predictor of school success. "Climate is the relatively enduring pattern of shared perceptions about the characteristics of an organization and its members" (Keefe, Kelley, and Miller, 1985). Teacher and student perceptions of school climate were systematically measured in the eight schools by the NASSP School Climate Survey. This instrument has 10 scales: teacher-student relationships, security and maintenance, administration, student academic organization, student behavioral values, guidance, student-peer relationships, parent and community-school relationships, instructional management, and student activities. The research team was able to draw several conclusions from the climate survey data and the information gathered during the site visits.

1. *Systematic monitoring of school climate, as perceived by students and teachers, is not a common practice.* Only half the schools visited had previously collected some type of climate data. Just one school had used a prior measure with known levels of validity and reliability (the Effective School Battery by Gary Gottfredson, 1984). In one school, the climate was studied by a team from a state university through the initiative of the superintendent's office. Other surveys were administered infrequently, typically as part of an accreditation self-study process. The data usually were not used in a systematic manner for site-based planning or school improvement.

2. *Teacher and student perceptions of school climate within a single school building can differ to such a degree that the views of one group may not be predictive of those of the other.* Usually (but not always) the pattern of teacher and student climate perceptions is similar; i.e., if one group is positive, the other group is also positive. In the schools studied, however, teachers were more positive in four of the schools while students were more positive in the others. In four schools, the differences in perceptions of teachers and students were great enough that further examination was warranted.

3. *Perceptions of school climate are influenced by conditions both internal and external to the school.* In all eight schools studied, there was little evidence to relate such variables as school size, student socioeconomic characteristics, or per pupil expenditures to perceptions of school climate held by teachers and students. If the principal or teachers or students perceived a lack of district or community support, perceptions of school climate were low. Regardless of these external influences, however, the most apparent internal influences on the perceived climate were (a) the philosophy of the principal and his credibility as the school leader, (b) the nature of teacher-student relationships, especially as perceived by students, and (c) the relative stability of the teaching staff within the school.

4. *School climate is perceived in a more positive manner when a school has an effective principal and administrative team, regardless of the leadership style employed.* Both a strong principal and administrative team are necessary for a positive school climate. If the principal was perceived as ineffective or about to leave the school, climate was low. School climate was positive when the principal was perceived as the leader of the school, and his or her philosophy, procedures, and mannerisms were well-understood by teachers and students and accepted as appropriate. Sample school principals varied widely in leadership styles, from "benign autocrat" to "manager by walking around" to "skillful delegator" or "participative manager." In schools with a positive climate, teachers and students reported involvement in decision making. Everyone knew how decisions were made and how to influence decisions.

School climate perceptions were most positive in schools with functional structures for planning and decision making and where the locus of decision making was within the building.

Satisfaction as an Explanatory, Mediating, and Outcome Measure

In NASSP's Comprehensive Assessment of School Environments (CASE) Model, teacher satisfaction is conceptualized as an input (explanatory) variable that may affect teacher and student perceptions of school climate and student productivity. The NASSP Teacher Satisfaction Survey is a job satisfaction instrument with nine scales: administration; compensation; opportunities for advancement; student responsibility and discipline; curriculum and job tasks; co-workers; parents and community; school buildings, supplies, and maintenance; and communication.

In the CASE Model, student satisfaction is treated both as a mediating variable that may influence other outcomes such as student academic performance, and as an outcome variable. The NASSP Student Satisfaction Survey has eight scales: teachers; fellow students; schoolwork; student activities; student discipline; decision-making opportunities; school buildings, supplies, and upkeep; and communication.

Data from the NASSP surveys of teacher and student satisfaction, and information from the site visits support the following generalizations.

1. *Student satisfaction is not a predictor of student perceptions of self-efficacy.* Student self-efficacy scores are reported in Table 5.1. These scores were obtained from the Brookover Self-Concept of Ability scale, which is included in NASSP's CASE Model. The self-efficacy scores are mean scores; the lower the score, the higher the reported level of self-efficacy. The two highest composite self-efficacy scores were reported for School #8 and School #1; yet these same schools were among the four with the lowest levels of reported student satisfaction. Conversely, School #6 had the lowest student self-efficacy score but the third highest student satisfaction score. One obvious explanation of this disparity is that student perceptions of their academic self-concept are not derived from their personal satisfaction with the school. Given the importance of both concepts, however, schools should probably continue to measure them to identify the need for appropriate interventions.

2. *Student satisfaction is most influenced by student relationships with teachers, and by opportunities to obtain needed services, to participate in the life of the school, and to receive recognition for accomplishments.* Student satisfaction was highest in stable schools with stable leadership and stable teaching personnel. In the two schools lacking these conditions (School #1 and School #7), student satisfaction was lower. No meaningful relationships were noted between levels of student satisfaction and such variables as

45

socioeconomic status, ethnicity, or nature of the curriculum. Particularly noteworthy was the lack of any predictable relationship between stability in the student population and the levels of student satisfaction.

3. *Levels of teacher or student satisfaction are not strong predictors of student achievement.* School #7 had relatively low satisfaction scores for both teachers and students, but its math and reading scores were relatively high. School #1, with the lowest teacher and student satisfaction scores, had the lowest math score and the second lowest reading score. School #5, with the second highest math and reading scores, reported the highest levels of teacher and student satisfaction. These findings are similar to those of many other research studies that have investigated the unpredictable relationship of satisfaction and productivity.

Both student satisfaction and student productivity are important school outcomes. Teacher satisfaction is also desirable, linked in our findings to teacher retention and stability. Because of the variable relationship between satisfaction and productivity, however, schools would do well to monitor both.

4. *Teacher job satisfaction is not related directly to the levels of expenditure at the school site.* When teacher satisfaction scores and per pupil expenditures were compared, no direct relationship emerged. Interviews with teachers during the site visits also reconfirmed a number of general conclusions reported in the research literature about employee job satisfaction. Compensation is an important factor in job satisfaction, but other factors are often more important; i.e., the relationship with one's supervisor, relationships with co-workers, opportunities to be informed about and involved in decision making, and opportunities for advancement. Caution is appropriate here. Studies often indicate higher levels of employee job satisfaction as chronological age or years of service with an employer increase. In most of the schools studied, teacher personnel were experienced veterans, both in the profession and in their school. One school with relatively low teacher job satisfaction was in the midst of a transition.

Many schools will experience, through retirement, substantial changes in personnel during the next decade. Planning will be needed in these schools to sustain teacher job satisfaction during these transitions. No clear recognition of this need was observed in any of the sites visited.

Productivity: Effectiveness and Efficiency

How effective and how efficient were these eight schools selected as representative of America's high schools? A number of outcome measures are included in the NASSP CASE Model to determine the effectiveness of a school: total achievement (combined math and reading scores); percentage of students receiving disciplinary referrals; percentage of students passing all courses; student satisfaction (NASSP Student Satisfaction Survey); student self-efficacy (Brookover Self-Concept of Ability scale); and, the percentage of students completing the school year (not dropping out).

The math and reading scores in Table 5.1 are reported as standard scores with a mean of 50 and a standard deviation of 100. Schools #2, #5, #7, and #8 have math and reading scores that are above average. School #6 is slightly below average, while Schools #1 and #3 have low scores.

The CASE battery incorporates the Productivity Analysis Support System (PASS) developed by Wailand and Authella Bessent and their colleagues (1984) at the University of Texas-Austin. PASS computes an efficiency analysis for each school. Data for the PASS variables are also reported in Table 5.1. The PASS score summarizes how cost-effective a school is in relation to selected productivity outcomes, given its levels of per pupil expenditure.

A careful reading of Table 5.1 suggests two generalizations about the sample site schools.

1. *An effective school may be either efficient or inefficient; an efficient school may be either effective or ineffective.* If effectiveness is considered primarily in terms of student achievement and satisfaction, Schools #2, #5, and #8 may be classified as effective. School #7, although efficient and high achieving, has relatively low teacher and student climate and satisfaction scores. School #3, with average scores for climate and satisfaction but low scores for student achievement, is efficient but not effective. School #6 has good scores for teacher and student satisfaction and climate but low average scores for achievement, and is moderate, at best, in efficiency. School #1 is both ineffective and inefficient.

2. *Student self-efficacy is important to school efficiency.* Self-efficacy scores contribute significantly to the efficiency of schools. In other research, student self-efficacy scores (self-concept of ability) are correlated with such outcome measures as student retention, student completion of an academic program, and student "willingness to try." An important function of schools, generally accepted in the American culture, is to maintain and increase the self-esteem of students. Increasing self-esteem probably contributes to a school's cost-effectiveness by decreasing the costs associated with truancy and remediation and improving student academic achievement.

Leadership for Effectiveness

Of the eight schools studied, three could readily be classified as effective. These schools were characterized by positive teacher and student

47

perceptions of climate and satisfaction and high student outcomes. These three schools included a blue collar suburban high school in a large metropolitan community, an urban school in a large city of 500,000, and a single high school serving a small city of approximately 25,000. The student populations in these three buildings ranged from 1,200 to 1,600. One of the schools was both racially and ethnically mixed. The second was ethnically but not racially diverse. The third was relatively homogeneous in racial, ethnic, and cultural characteristics. Data from these three schools and observations from the site visits support a strong central conclusion: *Effective schools have a strong principal and a functioning administrati ve team.*

Several common conditions prevailed in the three most effective schools of the study.

1. The administrative team met on a regular basis (usually once a week) but continuously engaged in informal consultation about the day-to-day needs of the school. Although a formal planning process was not used, systematic planning did occur through such mechanisms as periodic retreats and development of annual goals. Members of the team had specific responsibilities and the authority to carry them out. A collegial attitude prevailed among members of the administrative team and also among other employees of the school.

2. An advisory committee or council existed in the effective schools. These councils meet regularly to communicate about school issues, to plan ahead, and to respond to crises. These advisory committees or councils usually included counselors, coordinators or department chairpersons, and representatives of support personnel (e.g., health professionals).

3. The principal accepted, and was perceived as accepting, responsibility for what happened in the school. Principals were accountable. They were perceived as adept at seeking both formal and informal input from others and at delegating responsibility and commensurate authority. Assistant principals in these schools described principals' delegation skills with such phrases as "letting me use my own style" and "having total authority" to make appropriate decisions. One assistant principal said that his principal delegated authority more efficiently than any of the other five principals with whom he had served. Teachers in these schools reported well-defined relationships with the principal or another member of the administrative team and characterized the principal (or the team) as "knowing what is happening" in the school. A general feeling among teachers was that any problem or concern or idea could be brought to the principal or to members of the administrative team; that ideas were listened to and considered in decision making.

4. The principal was perceived as placing emphasis on productivity or success, often on measures of student performance mandated by external forces. Productivity was seen as "the name of the game" and satisfaction was perceived as "serendipitous," although "getting faculty to work together" was also a primary goal and indicator of success.

5. The principal and the members of the administration were perceived as a team, one that was proud of the school and visible in the school and at school events. Team leadership styles varied, depending in part on the principal's manner of delegation, but the team was evident to all and involved in all aspects of school operation. Input was readily given and feedback received. Communication flourished.

6. Tightly coupled or close supervision of instruction was not a common feature, but the more effective schools did have formal and/or informal input and feedback mechanisms that were more focused on instruction than in the less effective schools. Strong departmental structures were typical, with planning and supervision from a department chairperson, clear identification with a member of the administrative team, and frequent feedback from the principal. In one of the most effective schools, teachers reported both a strong department structure and clear instructional leadership by the principal. Clinical supervision was used for visiting, observing, and providing feedback to each of the teachers in this relatively large high school (approximately 1,400 students). By contrast, teachers in one of the other schools commented that their colleagues "teach pretty much what they want, leaving wide gaps in some areas while beating other areas to death."

7. Principals and other members of the administrative teams (including coordinators and department chairpersons exercising delegated authority) were perceived as placing emphasis on continuous professional development. Faculty involvement was emphasized in training and inservice. Even the effective schools, however, had some faculty members who resisted suggestions for improvement. One principal remarked that some of his teachers told him: "Don't bring back anything new. We have enough to do."

8. In the effective schools, students had relatively little participation in school governance, but felt that their views were considered. All three schools rated most effective had extensive programs for recognizing student accomplishments both in academics and activities. Student needs and concerns were major topics of discussion in the advisory committee meetings attended by our research teams during site visits.

Brookover and Lezotte (1977), among others, have reported school environments characterized by "a sense of dynamic tension," or "a sense of complacency," or "a sense of futility." These phrases seem apt for the eight schools visited. In the effective schools, a dynamic tension existed between past and present and future, with emphasis given to recognition of present accomplishments and a sense that "we can do better" and "we are, at least in part, masters of our own destiny." By contrast, other schools had a sense of complacency. "We're doing the best we can." Mechanisms for input and shared decision making were uncommon in these schools (e.g., advisory councils or faculty meetings focused on the improvement of instruction).

In one school of moderate effectiveness, the principal emphasized satisfaction and human relationships more than performance or productivity. No balance seemed to exist. The principal was highly visible. On a daily basis, he visited classes and often participated in teacher-led discussions. Positive feedback about classes and teachers was commonplace. Relationships were relaxed and informal, and the principal was described by teachers and students as "the most positive person we have ever met . . . . the best cheerleader we know." The principal's view of good teaching, however, was ambiguous. Standardized test scores were declining in the school, but teachers reported that the principal "understands that grades and test scores are not all the teacher's fault." In the final analysis, none of the principal's supportive mechanisms was oriented to instructional improvement.

Less effective schools in the study were characterized by problems symptomatic of a sense of complacency or futility.

- Administrators and teachers expressed concern that the community was not supportive of their schools and that little could be done to improve the prevailing situation.
- The principal of one school had little authority and autonomy to lead. The administrative team was fragmented and faculty involvement was lacking. One of the most respected teachers voiced the pervasive sense of hopelessness: "There is no direction in this school. If I felt better about the leadership, I wouldn't be taking early retirement. We (teachers) want to do better, to improve our programs, but the Board tells us, 'What you're doing is good enough'." Another teacher summed up the situation by saying: "I'm sick and tired of being sick and tired!" It was common practice in this school to reject personal or role accountability and to blame others while expressing the view that "nothing can be done."
- The "Candide Syndrome" was evident in two schools. ("Everything is for the best in the best of all possible worlds.") No formal or informal goal-setting activities were apparent. Visible and meaningful supervision of instruction was minimal and routine or unpredictable. The principals of both schools were viewed as instructional

leaders, but teachers did not go to them or other members of the administrative team (including chairpersons) for professional feedback. Data on student performance were not shared in any systematic manner to encourage faculty decision making or goal setting. Generally, a sense of complacency prevailed. One teacher epitomized the general attitude in both schools: "I suppose the principal is the instructional leader but we're doing all we can and we're doing a good job!"

To overcome these complacent attitudes, principals must work with teachers to increase data-based decision making. Schools can be both satisfying and productive. But what is more important, they can be *more* satisfying and *more* productive.

VI Summary and Recommendations

The high school principalship has been linked in recent years to school effectiveness and collaborative leadership approaches in the educational literature. Little research exists, however, on the formative processes of effective leadership. Are principals actually providing instructional leadership? Are they actually using collaborative organizational approaches?

The purpose of this study was to address some of these unanswered questions. Specifically, the study focused on three basic questions:

1. How are administrative teams organized and how do they solve problems and make decisions?
2. What is the administrative team's definition of instructional leadership and how is it operationalized?
3. How does the administrative team achieve optimum productivity and satisfaction in the school?

The plan of the study included procedures for school selection, data collection and analysis, and the cross-case reporting of findings.

Sample Selection

In past NASSP studies of effective principals and schools (Gorton and McIntyre, 1978; Keefe et al., 1983), subjects were selected by nomination of state and regional experts and school success evaluated solely on reputational factors. For this study, the research team used a sample of principals whose knowledge and performance of generic administrative skills were known from the NASSP Assessment Center program. The schools of these principals were profiled using the NASSP Comprehensive Assessment of School Environments (CASE) battery of instruments. Hence, specific information about both principals and schools was known and used in the selection of the sample and in the analysis of performance characteristics.

A purposive sample of 74 principals was drawn from the population of some 4,000 trained assessors in NASSP's Assessment Center program. These assessors were highly trained to evaluate potential school administrators in the 12 generic skills of the program. Thirty-seven of these principals were rated well above average in assessor skills (an "A" group). The remaining 37 were about average (a "B" group).

Methodology

CASE data were collected on more than 80 variables in 32 categories in all 74 schools. Data from 8 variables were used in the selection process to identify schools for site visits. Data from the remaining variables were analyzed for quantitative comparisons across schools, as reported in Chapter II of this study.

Eight schools were selected for site visits. Two of the schools were chosen because their selection variables established them as upper and lower benchmarks of the sample. The remaining six schools were chosen for interesting or anomalous factors in their selection variables. Each school was visited for three days by two researchers. Five prepared interview protocols were used to collect data from school administrators, teachers, and parents (as needed) on the three basic research questions. Classrooms were visited, student groups interviewed, and archival data examined.

After the visits, case studies were prepared according to a common format. The completed case studies were distributed to the members of the original research team for cross-case analyses of the three basic research questions. The results of these cross-case analyses are presented in Chapters III, IV, and V of this study.

Quantitative Data

The characteristics of the 74 sample schools were profiled on NASSP's Comprehensive Assessment of School Environments (CASE) battery. The principals of these schools were examined in two groups, those rated *above* average in assessor skills ("A" principals), and those rated *about average* ("B" principals). Subsequently, more than 80 variables were studied in 32 categories of the CASE instrument, including those dealing with goals, policies, regulations, personnel, and change.

Three variables were selected to measure school effectiveness: student achievement, student satisfaction, and student success. Achievement was measured by combining student scores in reading and mathematics. Satisfaction was measured by a specific rating scale in the CASE battery. Success was defined as the percentage of students passing all courses. All three variables were independent; that is, no correlation was found between them.

Because of school differences, achievement, satisfaction, and success were not utilized as direct measures of school effectiveness; rather, regression analyses were performed to predict expected scores to account for situational factors such as student population differences. Additional variables were retained only if proven stable over time and only if available from teacher and principal reports. Student reports of inputs were rejected as subject to possible misinterpretation since the effectiveness variables themselves were taken from student instruments.

Three variables were found (at or near the level of significance) to predict student achievement: (1) the percentage of students receiving free or reduced-cost lunches, (2) the availability of budget resources, and (3) the percentage of students in remedial classes. Four other variables were related to student satisfaction: (1) the level of teacher commitment, (2) the school's dropout rate, (3) the level of vandalism at the school, and (4) the age of the school building. No variables were correlated with student success which is probably a within-school rather than a between-school variable. Student success was eliminated from further consideration.

Schools were divided for analysis into three achievement and three satisfaction categories: (1) schools that scored above what might have been expected, (2) schools scoring below expectation, and (3) schools scoring at about the level of expectation. Schools in all three categories were examined by principal type, student achievement, and student satisfaction. Two two-way analyses of variance (ANOVA) were conducted—principal type by achievement and principal type by satisfaction—with the following results:

Principal Effectiveness. Differences in principal effectiveness were found in three areas: perceptions of school goals, participation in decision making, and reactions to change. Type "B" principals were more likely than the type "A" principals to support school goals that stressed: (a) increasing student skills, (b) increasing cost-effectiveness, (c) maximizing school time, and (d) increasing parent and community involvement. Type "B" principals were also more predisposed toward change, especially if the changes involved understanding student needs, soliciting input from those affected by decisions, evaluating programs, and conveying openness to suggestions. Conversely, type "A" principals were more involved in policy and program decisions. No other statistically significant differences were found.

Student Achievement. Given the large number of variables examined, differences in student achievement were few enough to have occurred by simple chance. The principals in the schools that scored at the expected level of achievement were better in directing student behavior and handling physical plant maintenance. The principals of these schools were also more likely to: (a) ensure adequate support services for teachers, (b) expend fewer resources on public information and community relations, and (c) enforce regulations on student employment. Principals of schools scoring below expectation spent more funds on public relations than their colleagues. No significant differences were found among the three categories of schools on any of the other variables.

Student Satisfaction. Again, statistically significant differences on this measure were so few that chance occurrence could not be ruled out. The principals of schools that were rated about as expected indicated strong district regulation of evaluation and instruction. Ironically, these principals also reported greater participation in policy decisions and program evaluation. The principals of schools that scored above expectation placed less emphasis on goals relating to athletics and on programs for exceptional and vocational students.

Principal/School Interactions. Comparisons of types of principals by the schools' expected effectiveness produced some interesting but confusing findings. In schools scoring at the *expected* level, type "A" principals indicated greater levels of teacher commitment than "B" principals, and heightened satisfaction for teachers and students alike. These principals also were more likely to report positive perceptions of school climate by both students and teachers.

In the schools that scored *above* expectation, type "B" principals reported higher teacher perceptions of school climate, and higher levels of student and teacher satisfaction and teacher commitment. Type "B" principals in these schools were more likely than their type "A" counterparts to be satisfied with their current programs, although they did place somewhat greater stress on programs for both special and college-bound students. These type "B" principals tended to emphasize student discipline while their type "A" counterparts stressed student attendance rules.

To further complicate the picture, in schools that scored *below* what might have been expected, type "B" principals were more likely to enforce student attendance regulations. These type "B" principals also reported greater staff understanding of students, more positive student and teacher perceptions of school climate, and higher levels of student satisfaction.

The quantitative findings, then, are not clearcut. Correlations between principal performance in assessor training skills and specific aspects of school effectiveness are not very helpful, especially when measured against expectations in particular situations. It would seem that either principal skill in assessment is not a good predictor of actual skill in school management or that principal performance is best judged only in the local school context.

The Administrative Team

The first major research question of the study asked, "How are administrative teams organized, and how do they solve problems and make decisions?" Interviews and other data gathered during school visits support the following generalizations on this question.

Team Composition and Functions. The administrative team always included the assistant principal(s) and often other staff members. The size and composition of the team generally reflected functional representation (departments, services, teacher roles, etc.). Some teams met regularly with formal agendas; others periodically or informally. Team members, especially assistant principals, were delegated authority in defined areas of responsibility (e.g., subject area supervision, scheduling or attendance, etc.). In every instance, principals reserved veto power over team decisions, but exercised it judiciously.

Problem-Solving, Planning, and Decision-Making Practices. The administrative team was the arena, in almost every case, for addressing problems and conditions in the schools requiring problem solving, planning, and decision making. Advisory bodies followed written procedures to identify problems and propose solutions for consideration by the administrative team. The planning process began with individual staff members and resulted in departmental and school plans that were strongly implemented and evaluated. Assistant principals and department chairpersons were given full authority in their delegated areas of responsibility and were supported by principals in making, approving, and following up on decisions. The more effective principals were both open to input and decisive in leadership.

Variations Among Schools: Four Underlying Factors. Every school in the sample confronted unique internal and external conditions. The administrative team coordinated data gathering and information sharing on these conditions to support efforts in problem solving, planning, and decision making. Four underlying factors determined administrative team success in confronting such local variations as school size, principal leadership style and proficiency, problem severity, and resource availability.

- Team success depended most radically on the *degree of autonomy* accorded the school by the district. Undue restrictions hampered and discouraged team efforts and wasted time.
- The *position power or prestige of the principal* within the school shaped the ability of the administrative team to act decisively on issues and problems or to become immersed in conflict. Effective principals set expectations, assumed control and established clear problem-solving and decision-making procedures.
- *The school-community environment* with its local values, expectations, and problems placed limits on administrative team action and success. Existing conditions such as low school-community esteem for academic excellence, severe security or drug problems, or conflicts over rules or procedures were often almost impossible to surmount. The principalship, at least in large schools, is too big for most individuals to manage. Even a team has trouble at times.
- *Staff member competence, diversity, and stability* conditioned the range of services and the quality of problem solving and decision making available to a school. The administrative team was most successful when staff members were proficient, insightful, and conscientious.

The Role of the Principal. The most effective schools had strong and creative principals. These principals, working with their administrative teams: (1) set the agenda and formed needed advisory groups and coalitions, (2) created a positive image for the schools, (3) pursued autonomy for themselves and the schools, (4) delegated authority at all levels, (5) brought innovative projects, training opportunities, and new resources to their schools, (6) anticipated impending issues and changes and planned accordingly, and (7) staffed creatively to achieve a diverse constituency in their schools.

Instructional Leadership

The second major research question was, ''What is the administrative team's view of instructional leadership and how is it operationalized?'' The main body of effective school's research and educational leadership literature has repeatedly emphasized the importance of instructional leadership. Site visits probed the issues of instructional leadership, its definitions, goals, strategies, and behaviors. Interview protocols and observation explored the nature of this leadership and how it was exercised in the schools.

What It Is Not. Instructional leadership is not a discrete set of behaviors or activities such as ordering curriculum materials, monitoring and evaluating teachers, or providing staff development. It is not just a responsible attitude to provide support for good teaching: adequate materials, a stable climate, good student discipline, and a general attitude conducive to effective instruction. It is not simply a philosophical bias, a written mission statement, or rhetoric about the importance of instruction.

What It Is. Instructional leadership is the initiation and implementation of planned changes in a school's instructional program, through the influence and direction of various constituencies in the school. Instructional leadership begins with an attitude, an expressed commitment to student productivity, from which emanates values, behaviors, and functions designed to foster student satisfaction and achievement. Instructional leadership is:

- *A Shared Responsibility.* The most common pattern was the administrative team providing support to department chairpersons who exercised functional leadership by working with faculty members in various departments. Chairpersons were often assisted by district supervisors or consultants.
- *Situational.* It hinges frequently on team or individual strengths in defined areas at a particular time in a specific place under a precise set of circumstances. It requires vision, flexibility, and common sense. It may be highly supportive or highly directive, depending on the circumstances. It may even fly against conventional wisdom.
- *Planned.* When planning was present, positive changes occurred. When no planning existed, no strategies were available, and nothing happened. The most sophisticated school possessed a long-range (five-year) plan, updated yearly with input from teachers, students, and parents. The process incorporated topical study groups, departmental and teacher objectives, and a total school plan.
- *Enhanced by a Common Purpose.* The most effective schools exhibited general agreement among all segments of the population about the primary purposes of schooling. These purposes were invariably *student-centered.* A willingness existed to sacrifice and exert great effort to improve instructional opportunities for students. These shared purposes promoted mutual respect and trust in the schools.
- *Involved in Risk Taking.* The more risks taken, the more people involved in risk-taking behavior, the better the outcomes. Risk-taking behavior is probably necessary because of the bureaucratic

nature of schools and school districts. Principals were regularly frustrated with their inability to deal expeditiously with problems unique to the local school. They were forced to "go through the channels." The more successful principals often bypassed the red tape or acted pending approval. They simply refused to let bureaucracy strangle innovation.

- *Characterized by Informed Behaviors.* Instructional leaders integrated attitudes and behaviors. They behaved in ways that would have a positive effect on teachers or students or programs. Leadership was goal-directed. All leader behaviors were directed to the improvement of the instructional program. Classroom observation, for example, was linked with discussion of specific instructional behaviors.

Essential Nature of the Instructional Leader

Several other qualities characteristic of instructional leaders were observed in our site visits. These qualities are more affective and intuitive than those discussed above.

1. *Instructional leaders know what they believe.* They work hard to stay abreast of issues and knowledge affecting schools and students, to form beliefs about these issues and facts, and to let these beliefs guide their decisions.

2. *Instructional leaders are aware of how important it is to start off right.* The leader's will to lead must be established relatively early if he/she is to challenge existing ideas and practices and assert useful control. Otherwise, considerable upheaval and interpersonal conflict can occur.

3. *Instructional leaders make decisions in the best interests of their primary clients.* They put student needs ahead of the needs of others—teachers, board members, parents.

4. *Instructional leaders do not ignore problems; they relentlessly seek them out and deal with them.* Real problems never go away. Leaders are problem solvers. They understand that the function of leadership is to solve problems, not avoid them.

5. *Instructional leaders pay attention to the little things.* Instructional leaders are not certified by simply doing their major, required job tasks. They are noted for their attention to detail and for caring actions.

6. *Instructional leaders earn their mantles.* The expectation that principals now perform as instructional leaders influences perceptions of their successful performance. Effective principals work to earn their mantles of leadership.

Satisfaction and Productivity in Schools

The final major research question was, "How does the administrative team achieve optimum productivity and satisfaction?" U.S. schools are expected to be *satisfying* places for students and teachers to work, *effective* in promoting student outcomes judged desirable by society, and *efficient* in using resources to accomplish these ends. The quantitative data collected by the CASE battery and the research team observations suggest complex relationships among satisfaction, effectiveness, and efficiency. But school success can be defined and measured in terms of these and related variables.

Influence of School Climate. Climate reflects school culture. If a school has a positive climate, its cultural norms and expectations are positively perceived. Teacher and student climate were systematically measured by the NASSP School Climate Survey in the eight schools visited. Several conclusions can be drawn from these survey data and from other information gathered during the site visits.

1. Systematic monitoring of school climate, as perceived by students and teachers, is not a common practice in schools. Only half the schools visited had previously collected any climate data.

2. Teacher and student perceptions of climate within a single school building can differ to such a degree that the views of the one group may not predict those of the other. Significant differences in teacher and student perceptions existed in half the schools visited.

3. Perceptions of school climate are influenced by conditions both internal and external to the school. Lack of perceived district support (external) and the principal's philosophy and credibility (internal) were powerful shaping factors in the schools we visited.

4. School climate is perceived in a more positive manner when a school has an effective principal and administrative team, regardless of the leadership style employed. Climate was positive in sample schools when the principal was perceived as strong, stable, and predictable. Leadership style was not a factor.

Satisfaction as an Explanatory, Mediating, and Outcome Measure. Student, teacher, and parent satisfaction with a school may be construed as an explanatory (or input) variable that affects climate perceptions and student productivity. *Student* satisfaction may also be a mediating variable influencing student achievement, and an outcome variable—one of the outputs intended by the school. Satisfaction and other data collected in the sample schools support the following generalizations.

1. Student satisfaction is not a predictor of student perceptions of self-efficacy. Student academic self-concept in the schools we visited did not depend on the students' sense of satisfaction with the school.

2. Student satisfaction is most influenced by relationships with teachers, and by opportunities to obtain needed services, to participate in the life of the school, and to receive recognition for accomplishments. Student satisfaction was highest in stable schools, with stable leadership and teaching personnel.

3. Levels of teacher or student satisfaction are not strong predictors of student achievement. The relationship between satisfaction and productivity was both inconsistent and unpredictable (confirming other similar research).
4. Teacher job satisfaction is not directly related to the levels of expenditure at the school site. Compensation was an important consideration in teacher job satisfaction, but other factors such as job relationships and advancement opportunities were more important.

Productivity: Effectiveness and Efficiency. Data from six outcome measures were collected in the sample schools. These measures of effectiveness were compared with other variables and also with the school's efficiency or cost-effectiveness. Two generalizations can be made about these relationships.

1. An effective school may be either efficient or inefficient; an efficient school may be either effective or ineffective. Both sets of conditions were amply evident in the sample schools.
2. Student self-efficacy is important to school efficiency. Increasing student self-esteem probably contributes to a school's cost-effectiveness by decreasing truancy and the need for remedial programs and by improving student achievement.

Leadership for Effectiveness. The most effective schools visited in our study had a strong principal and a functioning administrative team. Several common conditions prevailed in these schools.

1. The administrative team met regularly and consulted informally on a day-to-day basis. Systematic planning occurred and a collegial attitude was evident.
2. Advisory committees or councils were formed as needed and met regularly to communicate about school issues, to plan, and to respond to crises.
3. The principals accepted responsibility for what happened in the schools. They were adept at seeking input from others and delegating responsibility and authority.
4. Principals emphasized productivity and success. Faculty cooperation was encouraged as the basic foundation of success.
5. School administrators were perceived as a team that encouraged pride, cooperation, and communication in the school.
6. Strong departmental structures were evident, but close supervision was uncommon. Communication focused on improving instruction.
7. Principals and the administrative team emphasized continuous professional development and faculty involvement in training and inservice.

8. Student views were considered and their accomplishments recognized, but students had little direct participation in school governance.

Less effective schools in the study were characterized by problems and issues symptomatic of a sense of complacency or futility.

- Lack of community support.
- Lack of administrative direction and faculty involvement.
- Little formal or informal goal-setting, supervision of instruction, or regular communication and interaction among administrators and teachers.

Conclusions and Recommendations

A study of this scope uncovers many findings, some of which are anomalous and unhelpful, while others provide the basis for school improvement initiatives, future planning, or additional research. This second phase of *High School Leaders and Their Schools* suggests the following major conclusions and recommendations.

1. The relationship between principals' assessor skills and their skills in school management was not clearcut. The quantitative findings did not suggest any clear directions for school improvement or principal professional development.

2. The most effective schools had functioning administrative teams, and supplementary advisory bodies to assist in the problem-solving, planning, and decision-making processes. The team provided a focus for appropriate delegation of responsibility and authority. The more systematic these arrangements, the more effective the school was perceived.

3. The most effective schools had strong and creative principals. Enlightened leadership was fundamental to school success.

4. Administrative team success was limited primarily by the level of school autonomy, the position power of the principal, the school-community environment, and staff members' competence, diversity, and stability. Coordinating data gathering and information sharing on these conditions was the first and primary task of the principal and administrative team.

5. Instructional leadership was not an administrative monopoly. Neither was it simply an attitude nor a discrete set of behaviors or activities. Its primary focus was planned change in the school's instructional program through influencing and directing behaviors. It was most commonly exercised by department chairpersons with the support of the school administrative team and the assistance of district supervisors.

6. Instructional leadership was a shared responsibility, situational, planned, student-centered, risk-oriented, and informed. The most successful instructional leaders incorporated more of these characteristics.

7. Beliefs, beginnings, and best interests were characteristic of successful instructional leaders. They knew what they believed, asserted useful control early, and placed student needs above all others. They were also problem solvers and attentive to details. They earned their mantles of leadership.

8. A positive school climate was evidence of a functioning school culture. The climate of a school was perceived more positively if the principal was perceived as strong, stable, and predictable.

9. Student satisfaction with school was highest in stable schools, with stable leadership and teaching personnel.

10. Student self-esteem was important to school efficiency or cost-effectiveness. Well-functioning students very likely reduced school costs in truancy and remediation and achieved more successfully.

Final Impressions

A few lingering impressions merit further examination when the NASSP again studies high school leaders at the close of this century. The next study of the high school principalship should address these questions.

1. Have schools established truly functional administrative teams in the 1990s to support instructional leadership and school improvement?

2. Has instructional leadership changed in character? Has it been freed from current bureaucratic restraints? Have principals truly learned to be instructional leaders?

3. Have schools, since 1988, utilized systematic program evaluation to produce organized data for decision making and intervention planning?

4. What practices have schools adopted to facilitate the transitions anticipated from the large-scale retirements of educational personnel in the 1990s? Have these practices been effective in helping schools to retain the positive environments which have resulted, to a large degree, from people working together for long periods of time?

5. Have schools systematically monitored student satisfaction and productivity and achieved a balance between these two broad indicators of effective schooling?

References

Chapter I

Dwyer, D.C. "Understanding the Principal's Contribution to Instruction." *Peabody Journal of Education* 1(1986):3–18.

Georgiades, W.; Keefe, J.W.; Lowery, R.E.; Anderson, W.R.; McLean, A.F.; Milliken, R.; Udinsky, B.F.; and Warner, W. *Take Five: A Methodology for the Humane School*. Los Angeles: Parker & Son, 1979.

Gorton, R., and Kattman, R. "The Assistant Principal: An Underused Asset." *Principal* 2(1985):36–40.

Greenfield, W.D. "Developing an Instructional Role for the Assistant Principal." *Education and Urban Society* 1(1985):85–92.

Halderson, C.; Kelley, E.A.; Keefe, J.W.; and Berge, P.S. *CASE Technical Manual*. Reston, Va.: NASSP, 1989.

Hallinger, P., and Murphy, J. "Assessing the Instructional Management Behavior of Principals." *Elementary School Journal* 86(1985): 217–47.

Keefe, J. "The Critical Questions of Instructional Leadership." *NASSP Bulletin*, April 1987, pp. 49–56.

Marshall, C. "Facing Fundamental Dilemmas in the Educational System." *Education and Urban Society* 1(1985):131–34.

NASSP. "NASSP's Assessment Center: Selecting and Developing School Leaders." *NASSP Bulletin*, January 1986, pp. 1–58.

Ogawa, R., and Hart, A.W. "The Effect of Principals on the Instructional Performance of Schools." *Journal of Educational Administration* 1(1985):59–72.

Reed, D.B., and Himmler, A.H. "The Work of the Secondary Assistant Principal: A Field Study." *Education and Urban Society* 1(1985):59–84.

Trump, J.L. *A School for Everyone*. Reston, Va.: NASSP, 1977.

Walberg, H.J., and Lane, J.I. "The Role of the Administrator in School Productivity." *Studies in Educational Evaluation* 2(1985):217–30.

Chapter II

Schmitt, N., and Doherty, M. "NASSP Study of Measurement and Model Linkage Issues for the Comprehensive Assessment of School Environments." Unpublished technical report. East Lansing, Mich.: Michigan State University, 1988.

Chapter III

Anderson, M.E. "The Management Team: Patterns for Success." *OSSC Bulletin*. Eugene, Oreg.: Oregon School Study Council, 1988.

Haderman, M. *Team Management*, ERIC Digest Series, No. EA 25, 1988.

Wilhelm, P.M. "The Administrative Team, a Simple Concept To Facilitate Problem Solving." *NASSP Bulletin*, January 1984, pp. 26–31.

Chapter IV

Bird, T., and Little, J.W. *Instructional Leadership in Eight Secondary Schools*. Final Report. Boulder, Colorado: Center for Action Research, Inc., 1985.

Dwyer, D.C; Lee, G.V.; Rowan, B.; and Bossert, S.T. *Five Principals in Action: Perspectives on Instructional Management*. San Francisco: Far West Laboratory for Educational Research and Development, 1983.

Glatthorn, A.A., and Newberg, N.A. "A Team Approach to Instructional Leadership." *Educational Leadership* 5(1984):60–63.

Johnson, W.L., and Snyder, K.J. "Instructional Leadership Training Needs for School Principals." *Journal of Educational Administration* 2(1986):237–53.

Keefe, J.W. "The Critical Questions of Instructional Leadership." *NASSP Bulletin*, April 1987, pp. 49–56.

Keefe, J.W., and Jenkins, J.M., eds. *Instructional Leadership Handbook*. Reston, Va.: NASSP, 1984, 1990.

Murphy, J.F.; Weil, M.; Hallinger, P.; and Mitman, A. "Academic Press: Translating High Expectations into School Policies and Classroom Practices." *Educational Leadership* 3(1982):22–26.

Persell, C.H.; Crookston, P.W.; and Lyons, H. "Effective Principals: What Do We Know from Various Educational Literatures?" Paper presented at the National Institute of Education's National Conference on the Principalship, October 20–22, 1982, Washington, D.C.

Chapter V

Bessent, A.; Bessent, W.; Elam, J.; and Long, D. "Educational Productivity Council Employs Management Science Methods to Improve Educational Quality." *Interfaces* 6(1984):1–8.

Brookover, W.B., and Lezotte, L.W. *Changes in School Characteristics Coincident with Changes in Student Achievement*. East Lansing, Mich.: Institute for Research on Teaching, Michigan State University, 1977.

Gottfredson, G.D. *The Effective School Battery—Users Manual*. Odessa, Fla.: Psychological Assessment Resources, Inc., 1984.

Keefe, J.W.; Kelley, E.A.; and Miller, S.K. "School Climate: Clear Definitions and a Model for a Larger Setting." *NASSP Bulletin*, November 1985, pp. 70–77.

Pellicer, L.O.; Anderson, L.W.; Keefe, J.W.; Kelley, E.A.; and McCleary, L.E. *High School Leaders and Their Schools, Volume I: A National Profile*. Reston, Va.: NASSP, 1988.

Chapter VI

Gorton, R.A., and McIntyre, K.E. *The Senior High School Principalship, Volume II: The Effective Principal*. Reston, Va: NASSP, 1978.

Keefe, J.W.; Clark, D.C.; Nickerson, N.C., Jr.; and Valentine, J. *The Middle Level Principalship, Volume II: The Effective Middle Level Principal*. Reston, Va: NASSP, 1983.

Appendices

Schmitt, N., and Doherty, M. ''NASSP Study of Measurement and Model Linkage Issues for the Comprehensive Assessment of School Environments.'' Unpublished technical report. East Lansing, Mich.: Michigan State University, 1988.

Winesett H.D. Case Normative Study: PASS Analysis. Unpublished technical report. Reston Va.: NASSP, 1989.

Appendix A

NASSP ASSESSOR HANDBOOK
Dimensions Measured by Each Exercise

Generic Skills	Personal[b] Interview	In- Baskets	Likron Case Study	Scholastic Exam
Problem Analysis		X[c](E)	X(E)	X(E)
Judgment		X (E)	X(E)	X(E)
Organizational Ability		X (E)	(E)	X(E)
Decisiveness		X (E)		X(E)
Leadership			X(E)	
Sensitivity	X(E)[a]	X (E)	X(E)	
Range of Interests	X(E)			
Personal Motivation	X(E)			
Educational Values	X(E)	X	X(E)	X(E)
Stress Tolerance	X(E)		X(E)	X(E)
Oral Communication	X(E)			
Written Communication		X (E)	(E)	

[a](E) indicates the experts thought a particular skill dimension *was assessed* in this Assessment Center component.
[b]All skills were judged to be evident in at least some part of the interview; (E) is indicated for those for which judgments were most consistent.
[c]X indicates the *Assessor Training Manual* suggests that a skill be assessed by a particular exercise.

Appendix B

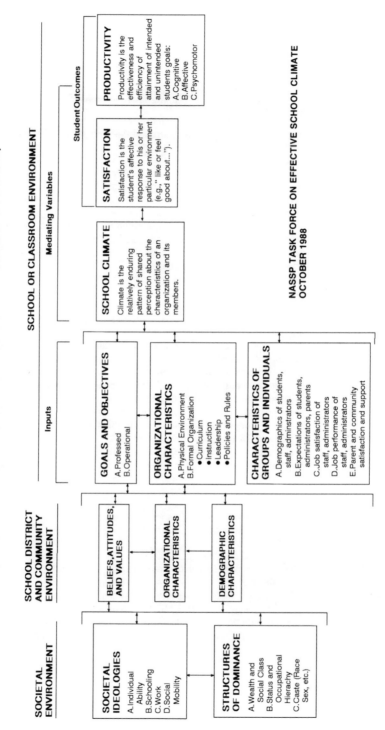

**AN INTERACTIVE MODEL OF THE SCHOOL ENVIRONMENT
(WITH SCHOOL CLIMATE AND SATISFACTION AS MEDIATING VARIABLES)**

69

Variable Listing of the NASSP Comprehensive Asessment
of School Environments (CASE) Model

The variables listed are those identified by NASSP's Task Force on Effective School Climate (November, 1988) based on findings reported in the national validation study of the CASE Model (Schmitt & Doherty, 1988).

	School District and Community Environment
POP	Population of the area in which the school is located.
SCHATT	Percentage of school-age children in the area served by the school.

	Input Variables
GOV	Whether the school is public or private, church-related or not.
MINORITY	Percentage of minorities enrolled in the school.
LUNCH	Number of students receiving free or reduced-price lunches.
REMED	Percentage of students in remedial programs.
BUDGRES	Number of activities for which budgeted resources are available.
ELECT	Number of elective courses in the curriculum.
STUDEXP	Average per pupil expenditure (exclusive of capital outlay).
CHGSCL	Principal's attitude toward change.
ADMINPERF	Performance of the school's administrative team.
TEACHSAL	Average teacher salary.
STRATIO	Student-teacher ratio.
PROFRAT	Percentage of school employees who are professionals.
TRANSFER	Number of transfers in and out of the school.
ATTEND	Percentage of students in average daily attendance.
SENG	Number of students whose primary language is English.
PHIERSCL	Principal perceptions of autonomy of action in the district.
PPARTSCL	Principal perceptions of participation in school decisions.
NOSTUDS	Number of students enrolled in the school.
SDRESRUL	Nature of student dress rules in the school.
SEMPRUL	Nature of student employment rules in the school.
GOALS	Importance of 14 selected school goals.
TSATSCL	Teacher satisfaction (NASSP Teacher Satisfaction Survey).
THIERSCL	Teacher perceptions of autonomy of action in the district or school.
TPARTSCL	Teacher perceptions of participation in school decisions.

	School Climate
TCLIMSCL	Teacher Climate (NASSP School Climate Survey)
SCLIMSCL	Student Climate (NASSP School Climate Survey)

	Outcomes
TOTACH	Total achievement (combined reading and mathematics scores).
DISPSCL	Percentage of students receiving disciplinary referrals.
PASAC	Percentage of students passing all courses.
SSATSCL	Student satisfaction (NASSP Student Satisfaction Survey).
SEFFSCL	Student self-efficacy (Brookover Self Concept of Ability scale).
STUDCOMP	Percentage of students completing the school year (not dropping out).

Productivity Analysis Support System (PASS) Variables
in the CASE Model

Nine of the 34 variables identified in the national validation study of the CASE Model (Schmitt & Doherty, 1988) also serve as variables in the Productivity Analysis Support System (PASS) to measure school efficiency or cost-effectiveness (Winesett, 1989).

	Outputs
MATH	Average student achievement in mathematics (standard scores).
READING	Average student achievement in reading (standard scores).
STUSAT	Student satisfaction (NASSP Student Satisfaction Survey).
SEFFSCL	Student self-efficacy (Brookover Self Concept of Ability scale).
	Inputs
ATTEND	Percentage of students in average daily attendance.
EXPEND	Average per pupil expenditure (exclusive of capital outlay).
PCTNONLUN	Percentage of students *not* receiving free or reduced-price lunches.
PCTNONMIN	Percentage of racial majority (*not* minority) in the school.
PCTSTABLE	Percentage of student transfers in and out of the school.

Appendix C

**Summary of CASE Variables Used
in High School Leaders and Their
Schools—Phase II**

Type of Variable/ Variable Name	Description of Variable
OUTCOME VARIABLES	
Student Achievement (ACHMNT)	Combined scores on tests of reading and mathematics
Student Satisfaction (STUSAT)	Degree of student satisfaction with school and learning environment
Student Success (PASS)	Percentage of students passing all courses
PREDICTOR VARIABLES	
Students' Economic Status (LUNCH)	Percentage of students eligible for free or reduced-price lunch
Budgeted Resources (BUDGRESS)	Availability of budgeted resources for programs and activities
Remedial Students (REMED)	Percentage of students in remedial programs
Age of Building (AGEBLD)	Age of building (in years)
Vandalism (VANDAL)	Number of serious vandalism incidents last year
Dropout (DROP)	School dropout rate
Teacher Commitment (TCOMMIT)	Degree of teacher commitment and loyalty to school and job
EXPLANATORY VARIABLES	
Principal Perception of School Goals	Increasing skills of students (GOAL1) Increasing breadth of courses offered (GOAL2) Enhancing school athletic program (GOAL3) Enhancing cocurricular activities (GOAL4) Upgrading staff development/inservice (GOAL5) Increasing programs' cost-effectiveness (GOAL6) Upgrading physical resources (GOAL7) Achieving racial integration (GOAL8) Developing methods to maximize time (GOAL9) Upgrading programs for special students (GOAL10) Upgrading discipline plans/practices (GOAL11) Increasing parent/community involvement (GOAL12) Upgrading academic programs (GOAL13) Upgrading vocational programs (GOAL14) (no importance = 0; primary importance = 6)

Type of Variable/ Variable Name	Description of Variable
Written Policy Statements for Attendance, Dress, and Employment	Student attendance rules (SATTRUL) Student dress rules (SDRESRUL) Student employment rules (SEMPRUL) Teacher/staff attendance rule (TATTRUL) Teacher/staff dress rule (TDRESRUL) (no = 0; strictly enforced = 3)
Principal Participation in Decision Making	Hiring decisons (PART1) Promotion decisions (PART2) New policy decisions (PART3) New program decisions (PART4) (never = 0; always = 4)
Principal Autonomy in Decision Making (PDMAUT)	Little done without approval Making decisions discouraged Small matters must be referred Must ask before doing anything Decisions must have approval (false = 0; definitely true = 3)
Resources Available for Programs and Activities	For needs assessment (PRIORRES) For student activities (MONITRES) For student discipline (DISCPRES) For instructional supervision (INSTRRES) For teacher evaluation (EVALRES) For staff development (DEVELRES) For program evaluation (PROGRES) For curriculum review and update (CURRRES) For review of instructional material (MATERRES) For school improvement plans (IMPVRES) For student recognition/reward (SRECRES) For teacher recognition/reward (TRECRES) For parental involvement (PARENRES) For public information & community relations (INFORRES) (no = 0; yes = 1)
Curriculum Guidance Supervision Provided	Curriculum guidance given by district (DISGUID) Curriculum guidance given by principal (PRINGUID) Curriculum guidance given by department chairman (CHMGUID) (no = 0; yes = 1)
Amount of District Regulation	District regulation of instructional methods (REGINSTR) District regulation of evaluation (REGEVAL) District regulation of curriculum (REGCURR) (little = 0; very extensive = 4)
	Degree of curriculum adherence required (ADHCURR) Degree of instructional adherence required (ADHINSTR) Degree of evaluation adherence required (ADHEVAL) (little = 0; very strict = 4)

Type of Variable/ Variable Name	Description of Variable
Administrator Performance	Curriculum and instructional leadership (PERF1)
	Coordination of student activities (PERF2)
	Direction of support services (PERF3)
	Directing behavior of students (PERF4)
	Staff evaluation and development (PERF5)
	Community relations (PERF6)
	Interpersonal communication (PERF7)
	Coordination with district, other schools (PERF8)
	Fiscal or monetary management (PERF9)
	Maintenance of school plan (PERF10)
	Overall evaluation (PERF11)
	(unsatisfactory = 0; exemplary = 5)
Principal Reaction to Change	Staff tries to understand student needs (CHANGE1)
	Try to find out how change affects relevant people (CHANGE2)
	Carefully evaluate our programs (CHANGE3)
	Staff effective in introducing change (CHANGE4)
	Mistrust between administration and faculty (CHANGE5)
	Administration and faculty often talk about change (CHANGE6)
	Administrators participate in school improvement (CHANGE7)
	Staff can propose change (CHANGE8)
	Students/parents can make suggestions (CHANGE9)
	Some procedures and programs need change (CHANGE10)
	Favor new programs that support the total program (CHANGE11)
	Favor new programs that can be implemented (CHANGE12)
	Uneasy about programs that are "new" (CHANGE13)
	Comfortable with current programs (CHANGE14)
	(strongly disagree = 0; strongly agree = 4)
	Reaction to defensible program change (CHANGE15)
	(very cautious = 0; strongly supportive = 4)
Principal's Tenure (PRINYRS)	Number of years principal has served at this school
Principal Turnover (PRINNO)	Number of principals in the last decade
Homes in Area with School-Age Children (SCHATT)	Percentage of homes in area with school-age children
School Professional Staff (SPROF)	Number of school professional staff
Racial Composition of the School (SWHITE)	Percentage of students who are white
Teacher Commitment (TCOMMIT)	Degree of teacher commitment and loyalty to school and job

Type of Variable/ Variable Name	Description of Variable
Teacher Stress (TSTRESS)	Degree to which teachers feel that job creates psychological tension
Teacher Adjustment (TADJ)	Degree of teacher adjustment to school, job, and colleagues
Teacher Participation (TPART)	Degree of teacher participation in personnel, curricular, and instructional issues
Teacher Satisfaction (TSAT)	Degree of teacher satisfaction with job and school
Teacher Climate (TCLIM)	Perceptions of teachers about how most people view the school
Student Climate (STUCLIM)	Perceptions of students about how most people view the school

Appendix D

Administrative Team Site Visit Protocols
Overview and Introduction

Purpose. The purpose of the second phase of the study is to answer three general research questions. First, how are administrative teams organized and how do they solve problems and make decisions? Second, what is the administrative team's definition of instructional leadership and how is it operationalized? Third, how does the administrative team achieve optimum productivity and satisfaction?

Method. The data needed to answer these questions will be collected primarily during a three-day site visit of eight secondary schools. Additional data will come from completed CASE instruments that were completed prior to the visit.

Structure of Site Visits. Each site visit will begin with a three-hour meeting with the principal of the school. During this initial meeting the research team members will 1) become familiar with the physical layout of the school (via a school tour), 2) secure information pertaining to the organization of the administrative team, 3) conduct a formal interview with the principal relative to the three primary research questions, and 4) set their agenda for the remainder of their visit.

Sometime during the visit the research team members will meet with each member of the administrative team, two (2) groups of 3 to 6 teachers in a "focused-group interview" setting, and, *as needed* for follow-up on ambiguous data, 3 to 6 members of a parent advisory group or school improvement council, also in a "focused-group interview" setting. Questions appropriate for use with administrative team members are included in the protocols that follow. Questions that may be asked of teachers and parents during the "focused-group interviews" are included in separate sections that follow this introduction.

Protocols. The emphasis of the research team members during the site visit should be on gathering information pertaining to the three general research questions. To aid the team members in their data-gathering efforts, however, a set of protocols has been prepared. Each general research question has been subdivided into a set of from two to four specific research questions. For each of these specific research questions, a series of questions that may be asked of various administrative team members (and others) to secure the necessary information are included in the protocols. Finally, archival data and exhibits that may be examined are mentioned.

Protocol for Research Question #1

How are administrative teams organized and how do they solve problems and make decisions?

Specific Research Questions	Prompts, Questions, and Probes	Archival Data/Exhibits
1a. What decision-making models are in place?	In schools today a wide variety of decisions must be made by administrators. Initially, we are interested in learning about the decision-making models and strategies in place in this school.	Written model(s)
	1. Is there a formal decision-making model in place? If so, is it written? If written, can you summarize it for me? If not written, can you describe it for me?	
	AS MODEL IS DESCRIBED PAY ATTENTION TO THESE QUESTIONS: WHO IS INVOLVED? WHAT ARE THE RIGHTS AND RESPONSIBILITIES OF THOSE INVOLVED? HOW ARE DECISIONS MADE (E.G., BY CONSENSUS)? HOW IS THE QUALITY OF CORRECTNESS OF DECISION JUDGED? IF NECESSARY, PROBE WITH THESE QUESTIONS!	

Sample
Decision-Making Model

Those powers or decisions not specifically assigned to any of the standing committees described below are reserved for the Principal of the school. The Principal may call meetings of any committee at any time in addition to the regular meeting times in order to discuss any relevant problem that may arise.

Legally, the Principal cannot abrogate his responsibility for the total school program. In essence, then, all powers or decisions assigned to specific committees are delegated and can be recalled by the Principal at any time for reasonable cause.

EXECUTIVE COMMITTEE

The Executive Committee of (name) High School will function as the ordinary policy-making agency of the school. The Executive Committee will consist of the following members:

Principal   Curriculum Administrator
Assistant Principal   Counseling Administrator
Vice Principal, Arts   Discipline Coordinator
Vice Principal, Humanities
Vice Principal, Sciences

The above persons will each have *one* (1) vote on the Committee. The consensus style of voting will be used. The Principal will retain veto power but will exercise it only with great advisement.

The Committee will determine its own rules and by-laws. It will meet weekly.

The agenda for each Committee meeting will be discussed and agreed upon as the first item on each meeting agenda. Any staff member may refer any matter for consideration to a member of the Executive Committee.

The Committee will make decisions on the following items:

A. Instructional problems, e.g., scheduling, staffing, etc.
B. Teacher-student relations
C. Student discipline problems
D. Inservice program
E. Evaluation program
F. Teacher-administration problems
G. Teacher and student complaints
H. Supplies, maintenance, budget
I. Pupil personnel program, attendance, grade reporting
J. Other administrative problems
K. Other instructional problems
L. Referrals from the Principal's Advisory Board

FULL FACULTY MEETINGS

The full school faculty will meet twice a month, or as needed. All faculty members will be expected to attend faculty meetings unless they are excused by the principal for a legitimate reason, such as having to supervise an interscholastic sporting event.

Anything that the Executive Committee or principal feels should go before the full staff shall be placed on the agenda. Other staff members may ask that items be placed on the agenda by conferring with the principal.

The full faculty will decide upon the following items:

a) alternatives that involve a major reorganization of the school
b) any item that a significant number of teachers (15 or more) wish to place upon the agenda
c) any changes in the decision-making model.

When feasible, meetings will be held before school rather than after school.

PRINCIPAL'S ADVISORY BOARD

In order to facilitate and encourage community involvement in the policy-making process of (name) High School, an Advisory Board with the functions of a standing committee will be established to advise the Principal and school staff. The Board will consist of the following members:

Principal	Volunteer Group President
Assistant Principal	Boosters Club President
Vice Principal (designated)	3 parents
Curriculum Administrator	1 area clergyman
Activities Administrator	1 District Junior High School Principal
Athletic Director	1 Member at Large (optional)
2 Teachers (Elected by faculty)	ASB President (student)
	Senior Class President (student)

The Board will meet quarterly, immediately before the Parent-Teacher (PTA) Meeting. Any interested party can request a board member to raise an issue of relevance to the High School (including student requests). Any Board member can ask that items be placed on the agenda for consideration.

The Board can *require consideration* of any issue by the Executive Committee or professional staff. Herein lies its power. The Board shall concentrate its efforts primarily upon the following issues:

1. Educational accountability to the school community, including cocurricular and extracurricular activities
2. Community relations, publicity, and public relations
3. Parent-school relations, including PFO Meetings, grade reporting procedures, adult education programs, etc.
4. Administrative and instructional procedures or problems
5. Budget and fund raising

Specific Research Questions	Prompts, Questions, and Probes	Archival Data/Exhibits
1b. What problems and issues have occurred recently and how have they been identified and addressed?	Problems and issues arise in a variety of areas: curriculum, student activities, personnel, and school-community relations. Can you describe for us a problem or issue that has been identified in the past year or two in any one of these areas?	Minutes of meetings; committee reports; focused-group interviews with teachers
	AS ISSUE IS DESCRIBED PAY ATTENTION TO THESE QUESTIONS: HOW WAS PROBLEM OR ISSUE IDENTIFIED? WHO WAS INVOLVED IN SOLVING THE PROBLEM OR RESOLVING THE ISSUE? HOW WERE THOSE INVOLVED IDENTIFIED OR SELECTED? WHAT SEQUENCE OF STEPS WAS USED TO SOLVE THE PROBLEM OR RESOLVE THE ISSUE? WHO WAS THE MOST INFLUENTIAL IN SOLVING THE PROBLEM OR RESOLVING THE ISSUE? WHAT WAS THE OUTCOME? IF NECESSARY, PROBE WITH THESE QUESTIONS!	
	Can you describe another problem or issue in another of these areas? (SAME AS TOP OF PAGE)	
1c. What are the formal and informal leadership structures in the school?	Will you describe for us the committee and departmental structures currently operating in your school (e.g., curriculum committee, faculty council)?	Agendas, minutes, faculty handbook, focused-group interview with teachers
	AS STRUCTURES ARE DESCRIBED ATTEND TO THESE QUESTIONS: HOW ARE INDIVIDUALS SELECTED FOR COMMITTEES AND COUNCILS? HOW ARE DEPARTMENT CHAIRS SELECTED? WHAT ARE THE FUNCTIONS OF THESE COMMITTEES AND COUNCILS? ARE THEY COMPOSED OF THE MOST RESPECTED FACULTY AND STAFF MEMBERS? IF NECESSARY, PROBE WITH THESE QUESTIONS!	
	Are there individuals in this school who, although not part of the formal leadership structure, are influential in the affairs of the school? Tell us about them.	
	AS INDIVIDUALS ARE DESCRIBED ATTEND TO THESE QUESTIONS: WHAT MAKES THEM INFLUENTIAL? HOW DO THEY OPERATE? DO YOU SEEK THEM OUT FOR ADVICE AND COUNSEL? IF SO, ON WHAT MATTERS?	

Specific Research Questions	Prompts, Questions, and Probes	Archival Data/Exhibits
1d. How are tasks assigned/How is authority delegated?	There are myriad tasks that need to be accomplished in any school if it is to function effectively and operate smoothly. Examples of such tasks include textbook adoption, student discipilne, scheduling of extracurricular activities, personnel evaluation. What tasks are you or your administrative team members expected to perform and accomplish in this school? AS TASKS ARE DESCRIBED ATTEND TO THESE QUESTIONS: WHO ASSIGNS THESE TASKS TO THE PRINCIPAL OR ADMINISTRATIVE TEAM? WHAT TASKS ARE ASSIGNED TO WHAT MEMBERS OF THE TEAM? HOW DOES THE PRINCIPAL DECIDE WHO ON THE TEAM WILL PERFORM THE TASKS? HOW MUCH AUTHORITY IS DELEGATED WITH ASSIGNED TASKS? HOW IS TASK PERFORMANCE MONITORED AND/OR EVALUATED?	Job descriptions; personnel evaluation forms; committee ''charges''

Protocol for Research Question #2

What is the administrative team's view of instructional leadership and how it is operationalized?

Specific Research Questions	Prompts, Questions, and Probes	Archival Data/Exhibits
2a. What is the view of instructional leadership?	Tell us about one of your major accomplishments in this school. (Of all your accomplishments in this school, tell us about the one you feel the best about.) AS ACCOMPLISHMENT IS DESCRIBED ATTEND TO THESE QUESTIONS: WHY DID YOU SELECT THIS ACCOMPLISHMENT? WHY DO YOU CONSIDER IT A SUCCESS? HOW MUCH DID IT COST? HOW DID YOU GET THE RESOURCES NEEDED TO ACHIEVE THIS SUCCESS (E.G., PERSONNEL, MONEY, MATERIALS, TIME)? IF NECESSARY, PROBE WITH THESE QUESTIONS! (NOTE—IF THE MAJOR ACCOMPLISHMENT DESCRIBED *DID NOT* PERTAIN TO INSTRUCTION—ASK:) Now, tell us a story about a success you've had in the area of curriculum and instruction. ATTEND TO SAME QUESTIONS AS ABOVE, PROBING AS NECESSARY.	Focused-group interviews with teachers

Specific Research Questions	Prompts, Questions, and Probes	Archival Data/Exhibits
	How would you define "instructional leadership?" LISTEN.	
	Do you see yourself as an "instructional leader?" How so? (What specifically do you do as an instructional leader?)	
	IF ANSWER IS "NO, I DO NOT" ASK:	
	Who in this school provides instructional leadership? (What specifically do they do as an instructional leader?)	
	Who are some of the best teachers in this school? What makes them the best?	
2b. What are the primary purposes of schooling?	Many people have been arguing recently over the question "what are schools for?" What do you see as the primary purposes of schools?	Written philosophy, mission statement, comprehensive planning documents
	Do you have an organized, comprehensive model or plan for achieving these purposes in this school? Can you describe it for us?	
	How did this model or plan come to be (e.g., historically, adopted, developed, adapted, mandated)?	
	How is consistency of purpose and practice across instructional program areas (e.g., English, science, vocational) achieved in this school?	
	What would you like to see achieved in this school in the next three to five years? What changes would you like to see take place?	
	How is consistency of purpose and practice across school levels (e.g., elementary, middle, high) achieved in this district?	

Protocol for Research Question #3

How does the administrative team achieve optimum productivity and satisfaction?

Specific Research Questions	Prompts, Questions, and Probes	Archival Data/Exhibits
3a. How is success defined and measured?	What are your measures of success for this school?	Summaries of survey results & test data; copies of survey forms and names and/or copies of tests; self-study & accreditation reports
	NOTICE WHETHER INDICATORS OF BOTH PRODUCTIVITY AND SATISFACTION ARE MENTIONED. IF NOT, ASK SPECIFIC QUESTIONS FOR EACH—What are your measures of productivity? What are your measures of satisfaction?	

Specific Research Questions	Prompts, Questions, and Probes	Archival Data/Exhibits
	Is there an ongoing process for study, evaluation, and planning in this school? Will you describe it for us? Who is involved?	
	Can you describe one or two changes that have resulted from this process in the past two or three years?	
3b. How are concerns for excellence and equity balanced?	Describe for us the students that this school serves.	Student handbooks; program and course descriptions; focused-group interviews with teachers
	AS STUDENTS ARE DESCRIBED ATTEND TO WHETHER SIGNIFICANT DIFFERENCES EXIST AMONG THE STUDENTS IN TERMS OF RACE, SES, ETHNICITY, CULTURAL BACKGROUNDS? IF NECESSARY, PROBE!	
	IF DIFFERENCES DO EXIST, ASK:	
	In what ways are teachers and students made aware of and sensitive to differences that exist (e.g., are materials on various racial and ethnic groups included in the curriculum)?	
	What provisions are made in the programs of the school to accommodate these differences (e.g., curricular, cocurricular, staffing, tracking)? What provisions are made for gifted and talented, remedial, handicapped students, and the like.	
	IF PROGRAM DIFFERENTIATION AND/OR TRACKING EXISTS, ASK:	
	How are students placed in particular programs or assigned to specific tracks? How often do students move from program to program or track to track? Are there incentives for students to enroll in more advanced programs?	
	When you examine your student test data, do you break down the data on the basis of racial, ethnic, SES, or cultural subgroups to see how these various groupings of students are performing? If so, what do you do as a result of the analysis?	
3c. How does the administrative team deal with increased regulation?	Tell me whether you feel more or less constrained in leading the school over the past few years. If so, in what ways?	Any external regulations
	As a principal, what pressures do you feel? What are the sources of these pressures? How do you deal with these pressures?	

Appendix E

INSTRUCTIONS TO RESEARCHER: Teacher Group Interviews

1. The researcher is advised that use of these questions for teacher groups is subject to a wide latitude of discretion. Questions may be omitted, used out of sequence, or adapted in any way the researcher feels appropriate.

2. At the end of this section, a set of answer sheets for the interview questions has been included. These answer sheets list the questions to be asked and provide boxes in which teacher answers may be tallied. In addition, a space is provided to record the group consensus, noteworthy comments, etc. A different set of answer sheets will be needed for each school visited.

3. For ease of administration, 6 (six) sets of reusable questions and answers have been prepared for members of the teacher group. These laminated sets should be distributed to the teachers to study as the interview is being conducted. Please remember to collect these sheets for use at subsequent visitation sites.

Questions for Teachers' Focused-Group Interviews
Part I

Problem Solving and Decision Making (Relate to Specific Research Question 1b) (Taken from Organizational Health Description Questionnaire: San Diego County)

	SD	D	U	A	SA

1. Problems are solved in this school.

2. Students are involved in decision making in this school.

3. In general, teachers' opinions are valued in decision making.

4. Faculty opinions are solicited.

5. Our school has procedures for identifying school problems.

6. Solutions to problems are actively sought from the staff.

7. Decision making in this school involves those wanting to be involved and those affected by the decision.

8. In our school, procedures have been established to evaluate our effectiveness in resolving school problems.

9. Describe instructional leadership in this school.

A	B	C	D	E
There is no centralized leadership for instruction. Teachers deal with instructional matters independently.	Occasionally, various people provide limited leadership. There is not an identifiable or consistent leader.	Instructional leadership is limited and is not a key factor in the school. The principal is *generally* the *instructional* leader.	The principal provides a degree of instructional leadership through coordination and delegation. The princpial is the instructional leader.	There is very clear, strong, centralized instructional leadership from the principal. Teachers turn to the principal with instructional concerns.

10. To what extent does the princpal promote the discussion of instructional improvement?

A	B	C	D	E
There is no real communication among teachers regarding the instructional program. The principal does not promote discussion of instructional improvement.	Discussion occasionally is initiated by the principal, but it is *not regular or planned*.	The principal or a committee initiated by the principal occasionally will plan formal or informal meetings to discuss instructional improvement.	There are meetings with teachers to discuss instruction. The principal is *active* in these meetings.	There are frequent formal and informal discussions concerning instruction and student achievement led by the principal. This is a *high priority area* for the principal.

11. To what extent does the principal demonstrate pride in the school?

A	B	C	D	E
The principal does not demonstrate pride in the school.	The principal demonstrates little pride in the school.	The principal occasionally demonstrates pride in the school.	The principal regularly demonstrates pride in the school.	The principal always demonstrates a high degree of pride in the school.

12. How often does the principal make formal classroom observations?

A	B	C	D	E
Once every two years or less.	Once a year.	Twice a year.	Three times a year.	Four times a year or more.

13. Describe the process of a typical formal classroom observation in this school.

A	B	C	D	E
There is no typical pattern. The principal stops in to observe classrooms and *may* follow up informally.	The principal generally informs teachers before an observation. A lesson is observed and feedback in some form *may be* given.	The principal and teacher may arrange for an observation time. Feedback follows the observation, *usually* in the form of a post-conference.	The princpal and teacher arrange a time for observations. Post-conferences follow *each* observation.	The principal and teacher plan the focus of each observation at pre-conference. An observation always is followed by a post-conference.

14. How often does the principal engage in a post-observation conference with you?

A	B	C	D	E
Once every two years	Once a year.	Twice a year.	Three times a year.	Four times a year or more.

15. What type of feedback or information does the principal provide after a classroom observation?

A	B	C	D	E
There is little or no feedback after an observation.	There is general feedback through discussion or a note. Feedback often does *not* focus on instruction.	The post-observation usually focuses on instruction in a general sense.	The feedback is primarily on instruction. Strengths and areas for improvement are generally discussed or presented.	The main emphasis is on instruction. The feedback usually involves the focus determined in the pre-observation conference.

16. Is the principal seen around the school? How often?

A	B	C	D	E
The principal is *not* visible around the school.	The principal can most often be found in the office. He/she is seen *infrequently* around the school.	The principal is *occasionally* seen around the school.	The principal is frequently and regularly visible at specific locations in the school (e.g., cafeterias, playground, office).	The principal is highly visible around the school. The principal makes many informal contacts with students and teachers.

17. Describe the school's requirement or policies concerning lesson plans.

A	B	C	D	E
The school does not require or monitor instructional plans.	The school expects planning to exist, but *seldom* collects or reviews plans.	The school requires planning and *occasionally* reviews these plans.	The school requires plans, reviews them regularly, and occasionally gives feedback.	The school requires and reviews plans regularly. The school discusses plans with teachers in relation to instructional strategies.

87

18. To what extent do you seek the help or advice of your principal in relation to instruction?

A	B	C	D	E
Very seldom or never.	Rarely.	Occasionally, usually related to some special situation or circumstance.	There are discussions about instruction with the principal, but the principal is not an important instructional resource person.	Instructional advice is sought frequently from the principal. The principal is an important resource for instruction.

19. How much weight does your principal place on the meaning and use of test results in instructional improvement?

A	B	C	D	E
The principal discourages test score analysis. There is a negative attitude toward standardized test results.	The principal is mildly interested or concerned with school test results. The principal may report the data, with no follow-up or interpretation.	The principal usually reports test results to the staff. There is little analysis or discussion of the data.	The principal views test results as somewhat meaningful and useful. The principal *regularly* reviews results with faculty to get a general picture of achievement.	The principal places much emphasis on the meaning and use of test results for program improvement. The principal reviews and interprets test results with staff.

20. To what extent does the principal hold teachers accountable for student achievement?

A	B	C	D	E
The principal does not discuss teacher performance in relation to student achievement.	The principal occasionally emphasizes to all teachers their general responsibility for student achievement.	The principal often discusses teacher performance in relation to student achievement. Some accountability is felt as a result.	Individual teachers' responsibility for student achievement is a priority of the principal. Individual teachers feel accountable as a result of this emphasis.	The principal frequently communicates to individual teachers the responsibility in relation to student achievement. All teachers feel accountable for student achievement.

21. To what extent does the principal promote a continuous staff development program in relation to instructional improvement?

A	B	C	D	E
The principal does not promote or arrange staff development.	The principal promotes programs mandated from above. The promoted programs usually are not related to instructional improvement for teachers in the school.	The principal *occasionally* works with teachers in promoting specific activities to improve instruction in the school.	The principal *regularly* arranges or promotes staff development activities for teachers in the school to improve instruction.	The principal is very active in securing resources, arranging opportunities, and promoting a continuous program of staff development activities.

22. To what degree does the principal arrange for coordination of the instructional program within and between grades?

A	B	C	D	E
There is very little or no coordination. The principal is not involved.	There is some coordination within and/or between grades, but not necessarily as a result of the principal.	The principal has arranged or allowed essential coordination between and within grades. There is some general coordination, but it is very loose.	The principal has arranged for coordination between and among grades. The instructional program is coordinated overall, but the principal is not active in coordination.	The principal and teachers work together to coordinate the instructional program within and between grades. The program is organized and well-coordinated.

23. To what extent do faculty meetings include discussions of instructional concerns?

A	B	C	D	E
Faculty meetings seldom if ever involve instructional matters.	General instructional matters will surface occasionally at faculty meetings. Instructional matters are *not* the *usual* or *planned* focus.	Instructional issues or activities *occasionally are included* as part of the faculty meeting agenda. These issues seldom are dealt with in depth.	Instructional issues are *often* the focus of discussions generated by the principal at faculty meetings. They are *often* part of the planned agenda.	Instructional issues are the primary focus of each faculty meeting. The principal consistently brings, or encourages others to bring, instructional issues to the faculty for discussion. There is evidence of instructional planning on the part of the principal.

Part III
Formal and Informal Leadership Structures
(Relate to Specific Research Question 1c)

24. Describe the committee and departmental structures currently operating in your school (e.g., curriculum committee, faculty council).

25. Are there individuals in this school who, although not part of the formal leadership structure, are influential in the affairs of the school? Tell us about them.

    (NOTE—MAY USE PROBES FROM PROTOCOLS ON 1c)

Part IV
Excellence and Equity (Relate to Specific Research Question 3b)

26. What provisions are made in the programs of the school to accommodate differences among students (e.g., curricular, cocurricular, staffing, tracking, gifted and talented, handicapped, remedial)?

27. How are students placed in particular programs or assigned to specific tracks? How often do students move from program to program or from track to track? Are there incentives for students to enroll in more advanced programs?

INTERVIEWER'S ANSWER SHEET
Teacher Interviews

Questions	Response Choices					Comments/Notes
1. Problems are solved in this school.	1. SD ☐	D ☐	U ☐	A ☐	SA ☐	1.
2. Students are involved in decision making in this school.	2. SD ☐	D ☐	U ☐	A ☐	SA ☐	2.
3. In general, teachers' opinions are valued in decision making.	3. SD ☐	D ☐	U ☐	A ☐	SA ☐	3.
4. Faculty opinions are solicited.	4. SD ☐	D ☐	U ☐	A ☐	SA ☐	4.
5. Our school has procedures for identifying school problems.	5. SD ☐	D ☐	U ☐	A ☐	SA ☐	5.
6. Solutions to problems are actively sought from the staff.	6. SD ☐	D ☐	U ☐	A ☐	SA ☐	6.
7. Decision making in this school involves those wanting to be involved and those affected by the decision.	7. SD ☐	D ☐	U ☐	A ☐	SA ☐	7.
8. In our school, procedures have been established to evaluate our effectiveness in resolving school problems.	8. SD ☐	D ☐	U ☐	A ☐	SA ☐	8.
9. Describe instructional leadership in this school.	9. A ☐	B ☐	C ☐	D ☐	E ☐	9.
10. To what extent does the principal promote the discussion of instructional improvement?	10. A ☐	B ☐	C ☐	D ☐	E ☐	10.

Questions	Response Choices					Comments/Notes
11. To what extent does the principal demonstrate pride in school?	11. A ☐	B ☐	C ☐	D ☐	E ☐	11.
12. How often does the principal make formal classroom observations?	12. A ☐	B ☐	C ☐	D ☐	E ☐	12.
13. Describe the process of a typical formal classroom observation in this school.	13. A ☐	B ☐	C ☐	D ☐	E ☐	13.
14. How often does the principal engage in a post-observation conference with you?	14. A ☐	B ☐	C ☐	D ☐	E ☐	14.
15. What type of feedback or information does the principal provide after a classroom observation?	15. A ☐	B ☐	C ☐	D ☐	E ☐	15.
16. Is the principal seen around the school? How often?	16. A ☐	B ☐	C ☐	D ☐	E ☐	16.
17. Describe the school's requirement or policies concerning lesson plans.	17. A ☐	B ☐	C ☐	D ☐	E ☐	17.
18. To what extent do you seek the help or advice of your principal in relation to instruction?	18. A ☐	B ☐	C ☐	D ☐	E ☐	18.

Questions	Response Choices					Comments/Notes
19. How much weight does your principal place on the meaning and use of test results in instructional improvement?	19. A ☐	B ☐	C ☐	D ☐	E ☐	19.
20. To what extent does the principal hold teachers accountable for student achievement?	20. A ☐	B ☐	C ☐	D ☐	E ☐	20.
21. To what extent does the principal promote a continuous staff development program in relation to instructional improvement?	21. A ☐	B ☐	C ☐	D ☐	E ☐	21.
22. To what degree does the principal arrange for coordination of the instructional program within and between grades?	22. A ☐	B ☐	C ☐	D ☐	E ☐	22.
23. To what extent do faculty meetings include discussions of instructional concerns?	23. A ☐	B ☐	C ☐	D ☐	E ☐	23.

24. Describe the committee and department structures currently operating in your school (e.g., curriculum committee, faculty council).   24.

25. Are there individuals in this school who, although not part of the formal leadership structure, are influential in the affairs of the school? Tell us about them.   25.

26. What provisions are made in the program of the school to accommodate differences among students (e.g., curricular, cocurricular, staffing, tracking, gifted and talented, handicapped, remedial)?   26.

Questions	Response Choices	Comments/Notes
27. How are students placed in particular programs or assigned to specific tracks? How often do students move from program to program or from track to track? Are there incentives for students to enroll in more advanced programs?		27.

Appendix F

INSTRUCTIONS TO RESEARCHER: Parent Group Interviews

1. Please remember that these interviews are *OPTIONAL*. They need not be used unless the research team feels, after gathering data from the principal and the faculty, that there is need of parent input.

2. If focused-group interviews with a parent advisory group *are* used, the research team must be especially vigilant against *hearsay evidence*.

3. Instead, whenever possible, the researcher(s) should probe for concrete examples of the principal's behavior. For example:

   "CAN YOU GIVE US AN EXAMPLE OF WHEN . . . ?" or

   "CAN YOU RECALL A SPECIFIC INSTANCE OF . . . ?"

4. At the end of this section, a set of answer sheets for the interview questions has been included. These answer sheets list the questions to be asked and provide boxes in which parent answers may be tallied. In addition, a space is provided to record the group consensus, noteworthy comments, etc. A different set of answer sheets will be needed for each school visited.

5. For ease of administration, 6 (six) sets of reusable questions and answers have been prepared for members of the parent group. These laminated sets should be distributed to the parents for study as the interview is being conducted. Please remember to collect these sheets for use at subsequent visitation sites.

Questions for Parent Advisory Group Interviews

	No	Yes, but	Yes
1. Does this school have a written statement of purpose that guides the instructional program?	No written statement.	Doesn't guide school decisions.	Written statement is the driving force behind most school decisions
2. Does the principal promote discussion of the instructional program and regularly report progress and problems in meeting objectives to parents?	The principal generally does not discuss instructional matters with the council.	Instructional programs and problems are not discussed on a regular basis.	Instructional matters are a primary focus of school improvement council meetings.
3. Does the principal help organize problem-solving task forces that include parent representatives to address instructional and other school needs?	There has been little leadership in setting up task forces.	Task forces exist in name only.	The principal provides leadership in organizing and supporting problem-solving task forces.

	No	Yes, but	Yes
4. Does our school's statement of philosophy reflect the belief that all students can learn regardless of home background?	Our plan anticipates that children's socio-economic status will be directly reflected in how much they learn.	We believe children from poor families have many learning problems and may not master basic skills.	Our philosophy is that all students can master basic skills as a direct result of our instructional program.
5. Has the parent advisory group discussed whether the standardized tests that are used measure the grade level curriculum being taught in the school?	There is little or no relationship between the standardized testing program and the basic skills curriculum.	There is only a moderate match between standardized testing and basic skills curriculum.	The standardized testing program is an accurate and valid measure of the basic skills curriculum in this school.
6. Are criterion-referenced tests or other teacher-developed assessment instruments used as a means of regularly assessing student progress in basic skills?	There is no systematic use of criterion-referenced tests or other assessments.	Chapter or unit tests are used occasionally to check skill progress; CRTs are mostly used for general direction and placement.	Criterion-referenced tests and other measures are used systematically to check student progress.
7. Is parent support and participation encouraged?	There is very little involvement or support of any kind provided for.	Parents are involved ony in the formal organizations like PTA, open houses, and school programs.	Parents are directly involved in supporting the school program, making important decisions as part of the school council, and volunteer in all phases of school life. *Most* parents are involved in a home and school support effort that promotes student achievement.
8. Do parents have opportunities to learn how to meet their children's needs and support the school's academic goals at home?	There are little or no parent education and support opportunities.	None of the parent education/support programs are directed toward parents assisting pupils in achieving basic skills.	There are regular and frequent opportunities for parents to learn how to assist their children in basic skills and to meet other parent-identified needs.

	No	Yes, but	Yes
9. Does the school stress parent-teacher conferences as a means to improve home-school communication?	There are no regularly scheduled parent-teacher conferences.	The conferences focus only on explaining grades and answering general questions.	At the conferences, communication is focused on factors directly related to student achievement and basic skills mastery. Plans for home-school support often results.

INTERVIEWER'S ANSWER SHEET—PARENT INTERVIEWS

Questions	Response Choices			Comments/Notes
1. Does this school have a written statement of purpose that guides the instructional program?	1. No ☐	Yes, but . . . ☐	Yes ☐	1.
2. Does the principal promote discussion of the instructional program and regularly report progress and problems in meeting objectives to parents?	2. No ☐	Yes, but . . . ☐	Yes ☐	2.
3. Does the principal help organize problem-solving task forces that include parent representatives to address instructional and other school needs?	3. No ☐	Yes, but . . . ☐	Yes ☐	3.
4. Does our school's statement of philosophy reflect the belief that all students can learn regardless of home background?	4. No ☐	Yes, but . . . ☐	Yes ☐	4.
5. Has the parent advisory group discussed whether the standardized tests that are used measure the grade level curriculum being taught in the school?	5. No ☐	Yes, but . . . ☐	Yes ☐	5.
6. Are criterion-referenced tests or other teacher-developed assessment instruments used as a means of regularly assessing student progress in basic skills?	6. No ☐	Yes, but . . . ☐	Yes ☐	6.
7. Is parent support and participation encouraged?	7. No ☐	Yes, but . . . ☐	Yes ☐	7.
8. Do parents have opportunities to learn how to meet their children's needs and support the school's academic goals at home?	8. No ☐	Yes, but . . . ☐	Yes ☐	8.
9. Does the school stress parent-teacher conferences as a means to improve home-school communications?	9. No ☐	Yes, but . . . ☐	Yes ☐	9.